STRANGEST MYSTERIES OF THE WORLD AND BEYOND

PART. I

EDWARD COLLINS

EDWARD
COLLINS

ISBN: 9798693827257

Cover design by: Edward Collins
Printed in the United States of America

CONTENTS

HIDDEN CITIES & LOST CIVILIZATIONS

- Atlantis

- El Dorado

- Lyonesse

Atlantis

Our knowledge of the world's most famous lost continent comes from the work of one man – Plato. The great Greek philosopher was the singular source of all information about the ill-fated island race and whilst experts write longwinded theses about the age and position of Atlantis, nobody is entirely sure that Plato did not just invent the Atlantean people as an allegory for what happens when a civilization over-reaches itself.

Despite this, the hunt for Atlantis is as fierce as ever. Plato lived in Greece between 428 and 348 BC, and revealed the story of Atlantis in his dialogues 'Timaeus' and 'Critias'. Many of Plato's fables were fictional creations used to illustrate a point, but the history of Atlantis was repeatedly stated as fact. The dialogues recount the story of Solon, a Greek scholar who travelled to Egypt in around 600 BC to learn more about the ancient world.

The Egyptians were known to have knowledge and records dating back centuries, and as Solon tried to impress his hosts with tales of Greece's achievements, the wise old Egyptian priests put him in his place. They revealed a story about a continent and a people completely unknown to him.

Around 10,000 BC, a powerful race lived on an island in the west, beyond the 'Pillars of Hercules', now believed to be the land masses along the coasts of the Straits of Gibraltar. The island was the kingdom of Poseidon, the Sea God. It had a huge central mountain with a temple dedicated to the deity, and lush outlying districts, there was an elaborate system of canals to irrigate its successful farms, and a bustling central city. The island was rich in vegetables, and was home to different types of exotic animals.

The Atlanteans were originally a powerful but fair race. They were an advanced people with a prosperous trading industry, a strong and noble army and a highly educated, cultured society. Their influence reached far and wide, and they controlled large areas of Africa, Asia and the Mediterranean.

Although the island left its inhabitants wanting for nothing, their taste for power and empire led to them over-extending themselves. An attempt to conquer Athens failed, and the Atlanteans retreated home to face a cataclysmic disaster.

Legend says that the great god Zeus saw the corruption that had seized the island's people, and sent down upon them an immense barrage of earthquakes, fire and water. Atlantis disappeared under the waves.

Whilst Plato's story was well known, the renewed modern interest in Atlantis began in 1882 with the publication of Atlantis: The Antediluvian World by a former US congressman, Ignatius Donnelly. Donnelly's book was a mixture of conjecture, misinterpreted fact and actual history. But there were some interesting ideas; he noted similarities in the science and culture of native races which apparently could never have met.

Likewise, the great ancient flood, which is said to have destroyed Atlantis, is logged in ancient writings and traditions of peoples around the world.

Exactly who the Atlanteans where is unknown. Some say they were aliens; some believe they were descendants of the Lemurians and some say they eventually travelled westward and became Native American tribes.

Similarly, the actual placing of Atlantis is a subject open to argument. Many experts suggest the island was actually in the Mediterranean, and a constant stream of archaeological investigations in the area has tried to prove this.

There are theories that Sardinia in the Mediterranean, and the island of Thera in the Aegean Sea, could be Atlantis. Both had highly-evolved civilizations: the Nuraghi people on Sardinia and the Minoan culture on Thera. Both also suffered terrible natural disasters. But neither of these islands are westwards of the Straits of Gibraltar, so to accept them is to doubt Plato's geography.

Also, the advanced races on these islands disappeared about 900 years before Plato – he stated that Atlantis became extinct 9,000 years before him.

Other experts say Atlantis was in the middle of the Atlantic, and all that is left of the island are its mountains, the peaks of which show through above the waves. These are now believed by many to be the Azore islands.

There is also evidence to suggest a huge comet or asteroid crashed into the southwest Atlantic Ocean many thousands of years ago and two 23,000-feet-deep holes have been identified on the seabed close to Puerto Rico. Experts believe the falling rock that caused them would have created massive natural movements, enough to destroy any mid-Atlantic islands.

Also, some say they have finally found the site. A perfect rectangle the size of Wales lying on the bed of the Atlantic Ocean nearly 3½ miles down lying 620 miles off the west coast of Africa near the Canary Islands.

So, where is Atlantis? Someday, we hope to have the answer.

El Dorado:

The story of 'El Dorado', the 'Golden Man'.

One of the first Spaniards to set off to find this fantasy land was Jimenez de Quesada. In 1536, Quesada and 500 soldiers hacked into the undergrowth from the northwest of what is now Columbia. After many hard days trudging through intense and dangerous jungle, they came upon two tribes of Chibchas, a race with plentiful riches.

They had gold, silver and huge amounts of emeralds, but they did not have the fabled 'El Dorado'. However, they told Quesada of a lake in the middle of a huge volcanic crater on the Bogota plateau not far away. The natives revealed that the lake was called Guatavita and each year the bizarre ceremony of the Golden Man would take place.

Tribal witnesses said the occasion was used to offer sacrifices and gifts to the god that they worshipped. The tribal king was smeared in sticky mud, on which gold dust was set. He and four other chiefs then sailed on a raft with their finest jewels and treasures, whilst the tribe played music at the shoreline. When the king and his party reached the centre of the lake they threw the offerings into the water, and the king then bathed himself to remove his golden covering. Quesada travelled to the lake, but could find no clue hinting at treasure.

As the years passed, each new expedition heard other versions of the El Dorado legend. Each one ploughed into the jungle certain they would find the wealth. None ever did, but they did come across other interesting things.

In 1537, one adventurer, Francisco de Orellana, was trying

to find the golden city by sailing down the Napo River. Orellana reached the end of the Napo, and realized it was a tributary to another, massive river. As he floated along this, a tribe of long-haired, fierce female archers attacked his boat.

The women reminded Orellano of the Amazons of Scythia in Greek legend, and he named the river 'Amazonas'. (The women were beautiful and exotic)

In 1584 another native rumor appeared. It suggested that Incas fleeing from the Spanish invaders had created a new city of gold called Manoa.

This became inseparable from the El Dorado legend, and in 1595 the British adventurer Sir Walter Raleigh attempted to find Manoa and its gold for Queen Elizabeth I. He failed, and a further fruitless expedition in 1617 helped to seal his execution. Over the years, yet another myth circulated – that of a lost mystical lake called Parima. It was described as being almost identical to Quesada's initial discovery, Lake Guatavita.

Despite this, more expeditions floundered in the jungle, haphazardly slicing their way through the foliage until they ran out of supplies, funds, men or patience.

Meanwhile, other Spaniards had decided to continue attempts at reaching the bottom of Lake Guatavita. In 1580s, Antonio de Sepulveda, a merchant living in Bogota, used 8000 native men to drain the lake by cutting a huge gash in the side. He did manage to remove a fair deal of water, and found considerable gold, but the earth walls collapsed, killing many workmen and causing the project to be abandoned.

Further attempts to drain the lake continued right into the twentieth century, and many historically valuable artifacts were found, but never the great quantities of treasure promised by the legends. There can be little doubt that, despite the countless and varied attempts hunting through the jungle, the Conquistadors never uncovered all the secrets of the Amazon.

Did the Spanish adventurers really find the lake of El Dorado? Or is it just another myth?

No one knows.

Lyonesse:

Off the very southwest tip of Land's End, in Cornwall, England, there lies nothing but water and a few small islands called the Scilly Isles.

Legend says that under the fierce Atlantic Ocean waves rests the remains of a beautiful old kingdom called Lyonesse.

It is a kingdom steeped in the legends of King Arthur and was once overcome by a great flood. Locals believe that if you look in the right direction at low tide you can even see the submerged towers and domes. Sometimes, late at night, it is possible to hear the ghostly tolling of lost church bells. Lyonesse is said to be a great country that contained magnificent cities and stretched to the distant west off Land's End, from St Michael's Mount to beyond the Scilly Isles.

There were supposed to be 140 churches in the country, and great forests covering the area. However, on 11th November 1099 a terrible flood raged over the land, drowning all but one of the inhabitants. This single survivor was a man called Trevilian, who saw the waves coming and rode his horse to safety on higher ground.

The Trevlyan coat of arms still shows a white horse rising from the sea, but the cities of Lyonesse were lost forever, and only the highest points of the kingdom peaked through the waves. At a distance of 20 miles from Land's End, we now know these summits as the Scilly Isles.

Another variation of the Lyonesse legend says that when King Arthur was wounded in his final battle against Mordred, the remnants of his foe's army chased the king to Lyonesse.

As Arthur and his men reached the highest points in the kingdom, the ghost of Merlin appeared. He called the terrible flood and Mordred's forces were drowned. It is said that Arthur then died on the Scilly Isles, and the association between King Arthur and Lyonesse has been extended by imaginative minds over the years.

Alfred Lord Tennyson even suggested the great king may have had his fabled, mystical court, Camelot, there.

So what proof is there to accompany these fanciful myths?

To begin with, surrounding St Michael's Mount at low tide, the fossilized remains of an ancient forest can be seen. So there once was definitely woodland under what is now sea.

Similarly, at low tide around the Scilly Isles, it is also possible to spot walls and ruins running from the islands' shores.

In the 1920s it was believed that structures found on the beach at Samson Flats were field boundary markers, although more recent thought considers that they were probably fish traps.

But definite remains of hut circles and cysts on other islands suggests the water really has risen.

Indeed, writings as late as the fourth century AD state that the Scilly Isles were one singular land mass. A group of rocks positioned halfway between Land's End and the Scilly Isles, known as the Seven Stones, are believed to mark the site of a once great city. Sailors and local fishermen call the area 'The Town'.

Some of these mariners have even reported catching parts of doors and windows in their nets around the area.

In the 1930s, Stanley Baron, a journalist from the London paper, News Chronicle was staying in Sennen Cove, just north of Land's End, when he was awoken one night by the sound of muffled bells. His hosts explained that he had heard the ghostly tolling of Lyonesse's churches.

Another reliable witness, Edith Oliver, was a former mayor of the town of Wilton in Salisbury. She claimed to have twice seen the towers, spires and domes of Lyonesse emerging from the waves as she looked out from Land's End.

Science, however, refuses to accept these legends. Oceanographers are convinced that in the last 3,000 years there has not been a big enough change in tidal height to account for any of these phenomena.

Unfortunately, there's no real, conclusive, scientific evidence. Despite that, people will continue being fascinated by tales of long, lost lands.

MYSTICAL PLACES

- *Easter Island*

- *The Bermuda Triangle*

- *Pyramids of Giza*

- *Puma Punku*

Easter Island

Easter Island or Rapa Nui, is in the south Pacific Ocean and lies about 2,300 miles from the west coast of Peru. Formed by a volcanic eruption on the ocean floor, it is separated from the other Polynesian islands by huge expanses of sea. The island itself only occupies 45 square miles, and has three volcanic craters.

Now lakes, they are some of the few areas of fertile nature, for the rest of the island is rather desolate and barren. However, it has not always been like this, and there remains evidence that the land was once rich in flora and fauna.

The first time the outside world knew about Easter Island was when a Dutch admiral called Jakob Roggeveen stumbled across it on Easter Sunday, 1722.

When he landed, he found a backward race which lived in caves and rudimentary huts, and practiced cannibalism. What truly amazed him was the huge stone carved figures, or 'moai', that stood on guard around the island.

Modern investigations have revealed there are something like a thousand of these great statues, standing between 12 and 25 feet high, and weighing up to 20 tonnes. The largest one is 65 feet tall and weighs 90 tonnes. However, when Roggeveen stepped ashore, many of these figures had been torn down by the fierce natives.

The origin of the Easter Island race is an issue of contention.

One early visitor to the island after Roggeveen was Captain

James Cook. Cook had a Hawaiian sailor aboard his ship who could understand the Easter Island native tongue. This suggested that they spoke Polynesian, and indeed the general consensus is that they were descended from a distant Polynesian tribe.

There is also a celebrated theory that they actually came from South America which is supported by the fact that bulrushes and sweet potatoes found on the island were said to be imports from that continent.

There were also considerable similarities between pre-Inca American cultures and the examples of Easter Island culture, although it is believed there may have been an early trading industry between Easter Island, South America and the Polynesian Islands.

The Easter Island race probably settled on the island sometime around the middle of the first millennium AD, and began building their statues quite soon afterwards. The early

Easter Islanders developed a precise technique for creating the stone men out of the walls of the volcanic craters. Using a system of logs and ropes, they would sit the moai on a funerary platform, called an 'ahu', under which the remains of dead elders were buried.

It is believed the stone figure acted as a talisman, guarding and protecting the clan of the dead islander, although some experts suggest the islanders ended up erecting the statues purely for the joy of making them. Archaeologists have also discovered wooden tablets called 'talking boards', which describe ancient religious rites of the old culture.

The Easter Island story is the archetypal island version of paradise lost. When the first Polynesian immigrants landed on the island it was a land of bountiful natural produce. There were great forests, sugar beet crops, exotic fruit and native meat sources. In these conditions the people flourished.

They built fine houses and enjoyed life, but in around AD 1500 a new cult called 'Makemake' or 'the cult of the birdman' sprang up.

This may have signaled the arrival of a new tribe from across the sea, and soon afterwards overpopulation and wasteful island management caused the crops to fail and the natural resources to be depleted. The different clans and tribes began warring, even overturning each other's statues, and legend on the island recounts a terrible battle between tribes of 'long ears' and a tribe of 'short ears'.

Within a couple of centuries, Easter Island was the barren waste populated by savages discovered by Roggeveen. The life of islanders only grew worse. The inter-tribal conflicts continued until 1862, when ships arrived and enslaved a thousand of the island's fit men to work in the Peruvian mining industry. These islanders quickly grew ill in the strange continent, and the few that returned home brought back diseases. Smallpox and leprosy reduced the native population to 111 by 1877.

Can we find the answer before the island gets destroyed into oblivion?

The Bermuda Triangle:

The Bermuda Or Devil's, Triangle is an area of ocean found off the southeastern tip of the United States. It is a region of water indelibly connected with mysterious vessel disappearances; the popular perception is that countless boats and planes have been inexplicably lost there.

The triangle extends from Bermuda to Miami and then to the Puerto Rico, and is said to contain a supernatural secret. Some high-profile disappearances have occurred there, and the notion of its existence has been turned into a modern myth in the media.1

Even the term 'Bermuda Triangle' was coined in a fictional publication.

But does the sea here really house some unknown power that pulls sea and airmen to their doom, or is this mystery based mainly on imagination?

The most famous loss in the triangle is known as the mystery of Flight 19, and happened on 5th December 1945. A squadron of five US Navy Avenger torpedo bombers set off from their base in Fort Lauderdale, Florida to conduct a practice mission over the island of Bimini. The flight contained 14 men, all of them students apart from the commander, Lt Charles Taylor. About an hour and a half after the mission began, radio operators received a signal from Taylor saying his compasses were not working, but he believed he was over the Florida Keys.

He was advised to fly north which would bring him back to the mainland. In fact, he was over the Bahamas, and his attempts to head north and northeast merely took him further away from solid ground.

A terrible storm that day hampered communications and it seems Taylor rejected a suggestion to pass control of the squadron to one of the other pilots. Radio contact was entirely lost and search craft were dispatched to try and find the flight to guide them back in. Of the three planes used to rescue Flight 19, one lost communication itself because of an iced over aerial, one was just unsuccessful whilst another seemed to explode shortly after takeoff.

Flight 19 itself has never been found, but it is assumed that they ditched into the raging sea when their fuel ran out, with the heavy planes rapidly sinking to the ocean floor. The US Navy recorded that the disaster was caused by Taylor's confusion, but an appeal by his family had this overturned, and a verdict of 'causes or reasons unknown' was given.

However, Flight 19 is not the only high-profile official loss in the area, and the USS Cyclops and Marine Sulphur Queen have also disappeared without trace.

The legend of Flight 19 was cemented by its inclusion in Steven Spielberg's Close Encounters of the Third Kind movie. Indeed, some theories state that visiting UFO craft enter an underwater base in the Bermuda area, and they have been the cause of the disappearances. Other fantastical ideas such as technologies from Atlantis or evil marine creatures have also been considered. Some people even suggest the triangle is the site of a gateway into another dimension.

Strange oceanographic features such as huge clouds of methane gas escaping from the seabed have also been blamed for the disappearances. In reality, the triangle does have one natural quality which may contribute to the losses.

Unlike everywhere else in the world – apart from the Dragon's Triangle near Japan – compasses point to true north rather than magnetic north. This may be a contributing factor to the triangle's legend, but the US Coastguard officially believes the losses are caused by a mixture of environmental and man-made mistakes.

This region is used by a large amount of ocean and air traffic, much of which is navigated by inexperienced pleasure-seekers. A strong Gulf Stream and unpredictable weather conditions not only cause vessels to run into trouble, but also remove many traces of them once they have been wrecked. It is interesting also to note that the coastguard does not view the area as having a particularly high incidence of accidents.

One researcher examined many historic losses in the triangle. He came to the conclusion that rumors and elaboration had clouded the real, understandable, causes behind the events. Similarly, the international insurers, Lloyd's of London, have records that demonstrate that this region near Bermuda is no more treacherous than any other waterway.

So are the disappearances, the lapses of time a direct effect of something sinister here? Or just another Ocean anomaly.

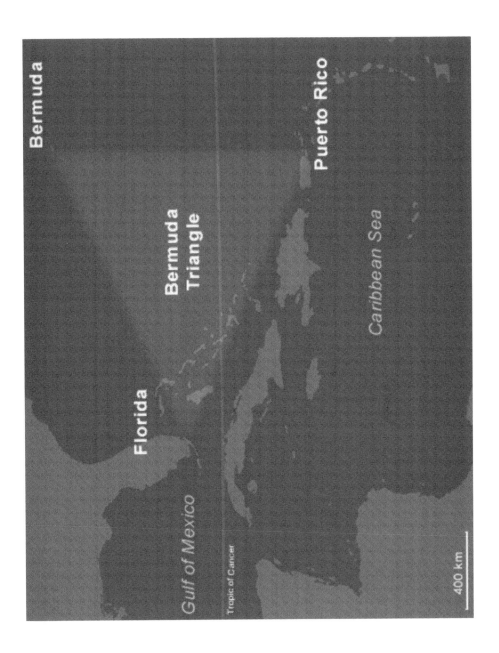

Pyramids of Giza:

The ancient Egyptians believed that after mortal death the soul or spirit would continue life in another dimension. They buried their Pharaoh kings, whom they regarded as living Gods, with all the treasures and objects needed to survive in comfort in the afterlife. They also embalmed their bodies to ensure that their mortal remains would be mummified and preserved for whatever fate awaited them.

Crucially, they built impressive burial structures to demonstrate the dead person's importance and to aid their ascendancy to the next dimension in the heavens. The most famous and enigmatic of these buildings are Egypt's pyramids, and the most mystical of all these is the Great Pyramid of Cheops at Giza. However, many people question whether the structure really is just a simple, albeit awesome, tomb or whether the design holds one of the great secrets of civilization.

The pyramids were erected between 2800 BC and 2200 BC; the first was built by King Zoser in Saqqara near Memphis. Although the structure was created with six stepped tiers, and is not a strict pyramid as such, it was the first building designed exclusively to house the property and remains of the king.

In the following centuries King Seneferu built his own trio of pyramids.

One at Maidum was called the 'False Pyramid' because it was abandoned mid-project due to a structural weakness.

One at Dahshur was known as the 'Bent Pyramid' because

of another design problem which meant the gradient of its sides had to be reduced as it was constructed.

The final one, called the 'Northern Pyramid of Seneferu', was built close to the 'Bent Pyramid', and is recognized as the first true pyramid.

The most impressive structure, however, was completed around 2500 BC for King Cheops at a site in Giza, ten miles south of the city we now know as Cairo. Using an estimated 4000 builders, and tens of thousands more manual labourers, the 'Great Pyramid' stands 481 feet high. It is believed it may have taken up to 30 years to quarry and assemble the two and a half million blocks of limestone, which weigh a total of six million tonnes. The base of the pyramid covers an area just over 30 acres.

It appears that great care was lavished on Cheops' structure, and although later pyramids were built for King Chephren and King Mycerinus alongside, neither is of the same quality.

Certainly, there are many fascinating aspects of the Great Pyramid's design.

Its sides run perfectly north to south and east to west to within a tenth of a degree. The base is an almost exact square, with an error margin of just seven inches, whilst the pavement around the structure is level to within an inch. Unlike other pyramids, this one houses a great number of chambers and corridors, with the lengthy 345 feet long Ascending Passageway running directly north. It had been widely assumed that the pyramid stood as a great monument to hold the body and treasures of King Cheops, although when the structure was first opened by Caliph Abdullah Al Mamun in AD 820 nothing was found inside. Al Mamun discovered the King's Chamber blocked by three huge granite plugs, which he and his men circumvented. But when they arrived in the great room, there simply stood an empty stone sarcophagus.

The mystery of what had happened to the pyramid after its completion, if it's assumed use is correct, has continued to this day. In the absence of real evidence of burial ceremonies in the structure, many fantastic other theories have grown. Some people believe it was built by God either as a stone version of the Bible, or as a record containing references to all events past, present and future. They believe that the various passageways represent historical time-lines, and intersections between them mark great happenings.

The birth of Christ and the two World Wars are supposed to be signified along these routes. Some experts who advocate this theory said it also showed a Second Coming in 1881 and the end of the world in 1953. Other mathematical studies of the Great Pyramid claim it demonstrates knowledge of the true value of pi, and was built using the 'sacred inch'.

A popular theory originating in the latter part of the last century is at the Great Pyramid was constructed by alien visitors. It has been proposed that these aliens did everything from creating Mankind to erecting the pyramid as a landing beacon for their next visit to Earth.

Another well-known idea is called the Orion Theory and was created by Robert Bauval and Adrian Gilbert. They believe the pyramids at Giza are an earthly representation of the three stars in the Orion Nebula. The shafts found in the Great Pyramid are supposed to correlate with important astronomical features visible at the time of the building's construction. The Orion Theory states that the Ancient Egyptians were direct descendants of alien visitors, and retained some of their knowledge. The purpose of these important design features in their tombs was to help point the spirits of the dead back towards the stars from whence they came. Many of these 'ancient astronaut' theories suggest the pyramids were built around 10,000 years ago, rather than the 5,000 supported by historians.

Other theories state that the instigating race may not have been aliens, but a now-lost civilization.

One writer, Edgar Cayce, was convinced the pyramids were built around 10,000 BC by travelers from Atlantis. However, his assertion that the Atlanteans also recorded the Second Coming of Christ in 1998 in the design of the pyramid, is somewhat flawed.

Some theories even suggest that our conception of the chronology of the pyramids is wrong.

Some people believe the build quality of the pyramids actually deteriorated, rather than improving, as the initial knowledge brought by the instigating race was lost over time. Although the Great Pyramid has been explored and studied more than any other ancient structure in Egypt, new discoveries constantly being made.

In 1954 a previously unknown sealed pit was found on the south side, containing a 140 ft long cedar boat, which may have been buried to help the king travel to the after-life. In recent years, space equipment and remote-controlled probes have been used to examine the building in ways never before possible.

However, NASA's refusal to publish underground readings taken by the space shuttle, and the Egyptian government's unhelpful attitudes towards deeper exploration, has only increased conspiracy theories and myths of hidden secrets.

For the world the mystery still remains unraveled.

Puma Punku

Spectacular in its own right, the Great Pyramid is, yet it pales in comparison to the ruins of Puma Punku in Tiahuanaco, in South America.

Tiahuanaco is in Bolivia, up in the Titicaca Basin, about 10 kilometers away from the great Lake Titicaca. The Titicaca Basin is high; 3,800 meters (12,500 feet) above sea level. Half is in Peru and half is in Bolivia, and right on the border sits Lake Titicaca. It's in a vast region of the Andes Mountains called the Altiplano, or "high plain", the largest such plain outside of the Himalayas.

The Tiahuanaco Culture predated the Inca, and their history is known largely from archaeology, since they had no written language that we know of. The earliest evidence of habitation dates from around 400 BC, but it wasn't until about 500 AD that the Tiahuanaco Culture truly developed. At its peak, 400,000 people lived in and around the Tiahuanaco site, centering on Puma punku and other important structures.

The ruins of Puma Punku are one of four structures in the ancient city of Tiahuanaco. The others three structures are; The Akapana Pyramid, the Kalasasaya Platform, and the Subterranean Temple.

Even with modern day technology and information, these structures defy logic, and confound those who seek to solve the mysteries that lie within them. The ruins of Puma Punku are said to be the most fascinating, and most confusing of all.

What Makes the Ruins Unique?

It is highly unlikely that any of the stones in Puma Punku were cut using ancient stone cutting techniques, at least not those that we are aware of.

The stones in Puma Punku are made up of granite, and diorite, and the only stone that is harder that those two, is the diamond. If the people who built this place cut these stones using stone cutting techniques, then they would have to have used diamond tools.

If they didn't use diamonds to cut these stones, then what did they use?

Not only were these stones really hard to cut, but they are also extremely heavy. One of these stone ruins weighs in at about 800 tons! These are big stones, and they are really heavy. The nearest quarry is at least 10 miles away from the site of the ruins. How in the world did these people move these blocks that weighed many tons, and how were they able to form a structure with them?2

With the technology that we currently have today, it would be extremely difficult to recreate the site of these ruins, if possible, at all. If we can't do it, then how did these ancient people accomplish this task? This could have taken place anywhere from 500 b.c. all the way back to the Ice Age.

The largest of these stone blocks is 7.81 meters long, 5.17 meters wide, averages 1.07 meters thick, and is estimated to weigh about 131 metric tons. The second largest stone block found within the Pumapunka is 7.90 meters long, 2.50 meters wide, and averages 1.86 meters thick. Its weight has been estimated to be 85.21 metric tons. Both of these stone blocks are part of the Plataforma Lítica and composed of red sandstone. Based upon detailed petrographic and chemical analyses of samples from both individual stones and known quarry sites, archaeologists concluded that these and other red sandstone blocks were transported up a steep incline from a quarry near Lake Titicaca roughly 10 km away. Smaller andesite blocks that were used for stone facing and carvings came from quarries within the Copacabana Peninsula about 90 km away from and across Lake Titicaca from the Pumapunka and the rest of the Tiwanaku Site.

These ancient people had to have been very sophisticated, knowing astronomy, geomancy, and mathematics. However, there are no records of this work. To build a place like Puma Punku, there must have been significant planning, and writing involved, but there is no record of any of this.

There is one more significant thing to mention regarding the ruins of Puma Punku. Not only were these stones cut somehow, but they were finely cut. The cuts on these stones are perfectly straight. The holes cored into these stones are perfect, and all of equal depth.

How is it that these ancient people were able to cut stones like this?

It is as if only master builders were allowed to come in and construct Puma Punku. All of the blocks are cut so that they interlock, and fit together like a puzzle. There is no mortar. There are only great stones that once fit together creating a structure some four levels high.

If these people could have moved these large stones to this precise location, then obviously they also had a way to place them one on top of another, but how in the world was this accomplished?

There is no answer to that question.

No one knows who designed and built this complex of sophisticated inter-locking blocks, and then vanished.

Researchers investigate the ruins on-location in Peru and present new computer analyses.

Forensic evidence on the ground, together with local myths and legends, suggest this site may have been designed and even once inhabited by a species of extraterrestrials.

One suggestion has been made that there had to have been some kind of ancient aliens who interceded on humanity's behalf, and our ancestors learned how to do all of this from them.

There are actual records of mythical origin, regarding gods and the part that they took in the creation of these places. Not sure how we have certain mythical records, yet no records of plans or writing that contributed to the creation of these places?

Another suggestion, is that a cataclysmic event such as a flood, wiped out these ancient peoples along with any records they may have kept. There is some evidence to support this suggestion. Perhaps these ancient people were technologically advanced at some point, and all but a few were wiped out by a major flood. The remnant would have had to start civilization all over again, and of course the ancient records would be lost.

Did they have advanced technology similar to ours, and then die off?

Maps have been found that would seem to support this theory. Maps such as the Piri Reis (1513), and the Oronteus Finaeus (1531), have been found that pre-date European discoveries. Not only are these maps precise, but they seem to claim that they are copies from even older maps.

These maps show the coastline of South America, rivers,

and even part of Antarctica which was not thought to have been mapped until 1818. These maps contain landmarks, as well as depictions of the areas which appear to be very accurate. Some people don't believe that these maps could have been made without flying over these areas in the sky.

Till the time, it clears up. This just adds on to be yet another unsolved mystery.

MYSTERIOUS THEORIES

- The Hollow Earth Theory

Hollow Earth Theory:

Could the earth, moon, planets and stars all be hollow bodies?

And very likely inhabited within?

If yes, what is Our Hollow Earth like?

The Hollow Earth Theory is one of the more outrageous contemporary conspiracy proposals. A massive intergovernmental cover-up would be required to substantiate its validity. Of course, the same has been said for alien abduction, UFOs, and government-sponsored psychic activity.

Essentially, Hollow Earth theorists' postulate that our planet is in fact hollow, as the name implies, with a crust thickness of 800 to 2,000 miles.

As ludicrous the notion of a hollow Earth may seem, remember that after several lunar missions, NASA asserted that our Moon may be hollow as it "rang like a bell" when impacted by rockets.

Most recently, this was affirmed when NASA scientists fired a rocket at the lunar surface in order to locate subterranean water supplies. Moreover, no one has ever drilled to a depth anywhere near the accepted limit of the Earth's crust. In fact, the concept of a solid iron core was largely conceived because it was the only cogent explanation for calculating Earth's gravity. Contrarily, theorists propose that within the hollow void is an entire civilization, illuminated by a small star at the center. Therein, advocates claim that the inner star or the crust itself provides sufficient gravity. It is believed that entrances to this subterranean world can be found at the North and South poles, as well as within major cave systems such as the Mammoth Cave in Kentucky, USA which has never been fully surveyed. This presumption would sound ridiculous if only there was no evidence.

Edmund Halley:

In a 1692 scientific paper, Edmund Halley – yes, he of comet fame – put forth the idea that Earth consists of a shell about 800 km thick, and of two inner concentric shells and an innermost core with about the same diameter as the planet Mars.

Halley did have scientific grounds for his rather bizarre thought-construct. It tried to explain why compass readings could be so anomalous: each of the inner spheres had their own magnetic poles and rotated at differing speeds. To compound his error, Halley proposed that the inner spheres might be inhabited and that the inner atmosphere was made up of luminous gases that, when escaping outward, cause the Aurora borealis.

Leonhard Euler:

In the seventeenth century, Leonhard Euler proposed a single-shell hollow Earth with a small sun (1.000 km across) at the center, providing light and warmth for an inner-Earth civilization. Others proposed two inner suns, and even named them: Pluto and Proserpine.

John Cleves Symmes Jr:

In the early eighteenth century, American John Cleves Symmes Jr supplemented the theory with the suggestion of 'blowholes': openings about 2.300 km across at both poles. Symes apparently was utterly convinced by his own theories: he campaigned for an expedition to the North Pole. The intervention of President Andrew Jackson was needed – to stop it, that is.

Quite unbelievably, the hollow Earth idea persisted into the twentieth century, when the study of plate tectonics and the like made it obvious that the Earth couldn't be hollow. Yet hollow Earth books and theories multiplied, many based on Symmes' work.

Marshall Gardner:

In 1913, Marshall Gardner wrote A Journey to the Earth's Interior, even built a working model of his hollow Earth – and patented it.

UFO's:

More recent theories suggest a hollow Earth inhabited by the creatures that fly UFOs across our skies, or by dwarves, dragons, other 'lost races' or 'ascended masters' of esoteric wisdom.

Some proposed new 'blowholes' are located in Mount Shasta (California), Mammoth Cave (Kentucky), the Mato Grosso (Brazil), Mount Epomeo (Italy) and the pyramid of Giza (Egypt).

The Shaver Mystery:

The pulp science fiction magazine Amazing Stories ran with a fantastic tale called the Shaver Mystery from 1945 to 1949. It entailed a series of supposedly factual stories by Richard Sharpe Shaver, claiming a superior prehistoric race had built subterranean caves, now inhabited by the 'Dero', their degenerate descendants. These 'Dero' uses the advanced machinery inherited from their superior forefathers to torment us on the surface of the planet.

Adolf Hitler:

The hollow Earth theory was quite popular in twentieth-century Germany; it's even claimed that Adolf Hitler gave the Hohlweltlehre credence in so far as that he ordered an expedition to spy on the British fleet by aiming cameras at the sky – a claim without historical proof, however. An even crazier theory holds that Hitler and other top Nazis escaped the Allies by fleeing to the inner Earth via an entrance in Antarctica.

The hollow Earth theory has a particularly strong hold on the imagination of writers (such as E.A. Poe, Jules Verne, E.R. Burroughs, H.P. Lovecraft and Umberto Eco, who have all used the idea in their fiction). A sub-genre postulating a hollow Moon seems to have died out after the 1969 moon landing.

Is it Agartha?

In some hollow Earth theories, there is a city or civilization at the core of the Earth called Agartha (sometimes spelled Agartha, Agharti or Agartha). This seems to derive from Aryavartha, which to the Hindus is the place of origin of the Vedas. An alternative name for this city is Shamballa (or Shambalah), which is Sanskrit for 'place of peace'. Chinese, Russian and Kirgiz folklore all have their own names for a similar place. Sometimes, both names are used simultaneously (as in this map), with Agartha designating the whole interior and Shamballa the main city.

Despite its age, the name of Agartha pops up in relatively recent popular culture, indicating that is was popularized probably only in the twentieth century. 'Agartha' is the name of a Miles Davis album, a song by Afrika Bambaataa, and is mentioned in Umberto Eco's book 'Foucault's Pendulum'.

No fly Zone over the North Pole:

Initially there was a no-fly zone over the North Pole but in Dec 2011, a decision was taken to allow the flights over the North Pole, dubbed Santa's short cut, is likely to cut flight prices, open up new destinations and reduce emissions.

How plate tectonics diffuse the hollow earth theory?

If the earth were hollow there would not be any reason for earthquakes. Earthquakes occur because the tectonic plates of crust float on a molten core and do one of three things in relation to the other plates...one is move away from each other (occurs in deep open ocean that forms ridges and troughs and makes the crust larger) second is one layer of crust dives under another and the molten crust then forms mountains eventually via volcanic action making the crust smaller) and the third is moving against another plate (forms mountains without volcanoes --Himalayas are an example and also decreases size of crust).

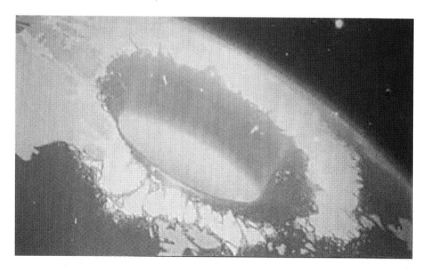

HAUNTINGS

- *Mary Celeste*

- *Ghosts of the Hampton Court Palace*

- *Waterworks Valley*

- *Bell Witch Mystery*

- *Lincoln's burial Train*

- *Amityville Horror & Spooky Franklin Castle*

Mary Celeste

The tale of the Mary Celeste is not technically a ghost story, but thanks to one of the finest fiction writers of all time the true story of this ship has passed into legend as one of the most perplexing of naval mysteries.

It was Sir Arthur Conan Doyle who, as a young writer, was commissioned to pen a tale about a vessel that had been found wandering across the Atlantic Ocean in perfect condition but completely crewless. He changed the name slightly, calling it the Marie Celeste, and added fictional embellishments.

But the facts themselves are strange enough and, to this day, nobody quite knows what happened to those aboard the Mary Celeste.

Originally called the Amazon, the ship was built in Nova Scotia in 1860. She was a 100-foot long, 282-tonne brigantine or half brig. Right from the start she was an unlucky ship: she suffered numerous accidents and ended up in a dire state of repair at a New York salvage auction in 1868.

The three new owners, James H. Winchester, Silvester Godwin and Benjamin Spooner Briggs, repaired and refitted the Amazon. They registered her in New York under the name Mary Celeste. Having been the master on three previous ships, Briggs took on the role as captain. Viewed as an honest, upright, God-fearing man, he was a captain who would only abandon his ship in the most appalling conditions. On 7th November 1872 the Mary Celeste left New York with Briggs, his wife Sarah, their daughter Sophie Matilda, and a crew of seven. Their cargo was 1700 barrels of American alcohol bound for Genoa in Italy.

A week later the British frigate the Dei Gratia left America to follow a similar route across the Atlantic. Captain David Reed Morehouse, who had dined with Briggs only a few days before the Mary Celeste left port, ran the Dei Gratia. On 4th December the Dei Gratia was 400 miles east of the Azores when its crew spotted a ship sailing haphazardly ahead of them. Through his spyglass, Morehouse could see it was the Mary Celeste as there was no sign of activity on deck, and no reply came to any attempt at hailing her, Morehouse decided to send off a boarding party.

Chief Mate of the Dei Gratia, Oliver Deveau, was dispatched as leader of the group who set off in a small boat. He found the ship in a perfectly seaworthy condition with good supplies of food and water, but with a certain amount of interior damage. There was a great deal of water over the ship's decks, and one of the pumps was broken. The galley stove had moved from its correct position, and the ship's clock and compass were also damaged.

The crew appeared to have left quickly, as their waterproof boots and pipes were still on board, but it looked as though Captain Briggs had taken the chronometer and sextant. Deveau noticed that there were no lifeboats left on the ship. The most interesting find was the ship's log. The last entry was dated 24th November, when the Mary Celeste was only just passing the Azores. That meant the ship had sailed itself for over 400 miles on a perfectly-plotted course for the Mediterranean. The crew of the Dei Gratia now split into two groups. One stayed on their own ship, whilst the other sailed the Mary Celeste onto Gibraltar. The cargo of alcohol reached Genoa with only nine barrels damaged.

Following a naval inquiry, the Mary Celeste was sold on and then continued to change hands frequently. After hearing her history, many mariners decided that she was not the sort of ship they were too keen on.

In 1884 she was wrecked off the coast of Haiti in an alleged insurance scam.

But what happened to her crew in 1872?

The official version of events, arrived at by the British and American authorities, was that the crew had mutinied and then abandoned ship. This seems very unlikely as it was only a short journey and there were no signs of a struggle on board.

Also, Briggs was generally viewed as a decent and respected captain.

A second theory is almost completely implausible. It came from a man called Fosdyk who left papers after his death saying he was a secret passenger on the Mary Celeste. He claimed that Briggs had constructed a special deck in the bow for his daughter. During the voyage, two of the crew were having a swimming race around the boat when one man was attacked by sharks. As the rest of the ship's passengers crowded onto the little girl's deck to see what was happening, the temporary structure gave way, sending all those on board into the sea and to the sharks. Fosdyk claimed to have survived by clinging to a piece of driftwood.

The most probable explanation, given the facts, was that the Mary Celeste hit a terrible patch of bad weather. As the ship bucked on the waves, some alcohol spilled from the cargo barrels, covering the hold floor. Coupled with this, the ship's movement caused the galley stove to become unstable.

Fearing the ship was about to explode, Briggs ordered everybody into the lifeboat, and planned to follow behind the Mary Celeste attached to the ship's main halyard, a strong, thick rope.

As the storm worsened, somehow the halyard snapped and the Mary Celeste sailed off. Briggs, his family and crew were left stranded in a small boat in the middle of the Atlantic Ocean. There is some evidence for this scenario. Morehouse testified that the Dei Gratia had been battered in severe storms during the days leading up to finding the Mary Celeste. As mentioned earlier, Deveau noticed alcohol and water spilled over the boards of the ship, whilst the galley and its stove were found in a very disorderly condition.

Crucially, Deveau also noted that all small boats were missing, and the halyard was found dangling, frayed and split, over the side of the ship. Ghost ships were not particularly rare during the nineteenth century. The Dutch schooner Hermania and the ship Marathon were both found abandoned but floating in perfect order around the same time as the Mary Celeste.

However, with the help of Conan Doyle, it was the Mary Celeste that really caught the public's interest. Whilst his, and our, imagination can come up with possibilities, the true fate of the souls aboard the Mary Celeste is something we will probably never know.

Ghosts of the Hampton Court Palace

Hampton Court Palace on the banks of the River Thames, just outside London, is said to be the most haunted royal building in Britain.

Most palaces and castles are known to house a few mythical spectres, but the special quality about Hampton Court is the sheer range of apparitions.

From wives of King Henry VIII, to Cavalier soldiers, to a ghostly dog, the palace is plagued by over a dozen unexplained phenomena.

Hampton Court was originally bought by Cardinal Wolsey, but Henry VIII liked the building and took it as his own. Henry was the first person to report seeing the decapitated head of his second wife, Anne Boleyn, who was executed for treasonous adultery in 1536. Subsequent sightings of her have described her with, without and even carrying her head. Witnesses say she appears in blue or black, walking slowly, looking angry or upset, and is said to pervade a sense of grief or despair.

Henry's third wife, Jane Seymour, reportedly the love of his life, was the only wife to be buried alongside him in his death vault She died giving birth to his only son, Edward, in 1537 and was the only one of his queens to die of natural causes before Henry. It is said that on the anniversary of Edward's birth, 12th October, Lady Jane appears from the Queen's Apartments and walks round to the Silver Stick Gallery. Witnesses say the apparition wears a white robe and carries a lit candle.

With Jane's death, Henry's new-born son was entrusted to the care of a nursemaid, Sibell Penn. Penn died of smallpox in 1562 and was buried in St Mary's Church, not far from the palace in Hampton. Her spirit was not seen or heard from until the 1820s when St Mary's Church was stuck by lightning and during the rebuilding, Penn's remains were removed to another grave. Since then there have been reports of a tall, hooded figure known as the 'Grey Lady' walking the corridors of the palace at the same time as a strange spinning noise was heard in the west wing of the building. The whirring sound seemed to be coming from an odd wall of a corridor, so during investigations the wall was knocked down. Behind it they found a previously unknown room, along with Sibell Penn's old spinning wheel.

Undoubtedly the most celebrated ghost in Hampton Court can be found in what is called the Haunted Gallery. The ghost is that of Henry's fifth wife, Catherine Howard, who was beheaded in 1542 for infidelity with younger men. Legend has it that the moments following the ordering of her execution can be seen played out by specters in the gallery. Witnesses say Catherine's figure appears screaming for her life, until guards seize her and drag her away. Some people have also seen her trying to find sanctuary in the palace chapel, whilst a palace warder once reported seeing a ghostly hand wearing one of Catherine's heavily jewelled rings knocking on the chapel door.

Not all the restless spirits that wander the hallways of the palace are of royal lineage. Palace staff have seen a strange grey mist floating along the kitchen floor, and a guard reported seeing a dark, male figure wearing a top hat who just disappeared into the wine cellar. (Witnesses said it was strange, as he looked more like a spirit man!) There are also tales of a ghostly dog being seen entering the King's Apartments.

Many people have reported seeing two noisy figures fighting in the main courtyard. During renovation work in the yard, the skeletons of two English Civil War Cavalier soldiers were found and given a proper burial. There have been no sightings of the figures since.

A group of seven women and two men dressed in old-fashioned clothing are also said to wander Hampton Court.

In 1917 police officer even opened a door for these apparitions, before they simply disappeared into thin air.

Nowadays, visitors to the palace should not be concerned if they see some strange characters in period dress, for many of the specialist guides giving tours of the building now appear in costume.

Fascinating, eh!

Waterworks Valley:

Waterworks Valley, in the parish of St Lawrence in the Channel Island of Jersey, is named after the great number of reservoirs and pumping stations found along it.

Even in the daytime, it is a brooding, haunting place, overcast as it is by a thick layer of trees and foliage. It is damp and dark, and people are often forgiven for seeing or hearing things.

Sometimes there is no mistaking the ghostly sights and sounds that occur. Countless people have seen it pass by, and even more have run away after hearing it approach.

This, they say, is the 'Phantom Carriage'. The stories often follow a similar pattern. Usually the events occur in the evening and begin with the muffled ringing of bells – the unearthly music is said to sound more like wedding bells than anything sombre. Gradually, mixed with ringing, another noise becomes discernible. It is the sound of horses trotting along the valley, accompanied by the spinning, bumping rattles of a carriage.

Emerging from the gloom, witnesses spot the procession which is clothed in eighteenth century costume. They see that the coach's passenger is a bride in her wedding dress, but as it rolls past witnesses see the face behind the veil. It is the haggard skull of a corpse.

One tale of explanation claims that in the early eighteenth century a girl who was due to be married at St Lawrence parish church was disappointed at the altar. It is said she committed suicide that evening, and the apparition is a representation of her timeless sorrow.

Another variation of the story is that she committed suicide on the eve of the wedding, but her ghostly figure appeared at the church the next day anyway. It was only as the groom lifted the veil that he noticed the pale lifeless face of a corpse underneath.

Many people believe the phenomenon happens only once a year at a specific time. But there are so many sightings, and such vivid recollections, that perhaps the girl's misery is constant and never-ending.

Bell Witch Mystery

John Bell, a farmer from North Carolina, along with his wife and children settled in northern Robertson County Tennessee in 1804. Their farm consisted of 320 acres of rich farm land that laid along the Red River. They lived a quite peaceful life here for the first 13 years. They were members of the Red River Baptist Church where John became a deacon. The family grew and became somewhat prosperous.

In the late summer of 1817, something would happen that would change their lives forever. Some members of the family began seeing strange looking animals around the property. Then late at night they started hearing knocking sounds on the doors and outer walls of the house. Later sounds were being heard in the house. Sounds of a rat gnawing on the bed post, chains being drug through the house, stones being dropped on the wooden floors, then gulping and choking sounds.

The family was terrified but kept the problem to themselves for over a year. When things became intolerable John confided in a neighbor, James Johnson. He invited Mr. and Mrs. Johnson to spend the night. After several nights of witnessing these strange things, Mr. Johnson suggested that more people should be told. And a committee was formed and an investigation started.

It was not long before people were coming from miles around to hear and witness this unseen force that was terrorizing the Bell home. Before long, this unseen force had gained enough strength that it now had a voice. When asked who and what it was, it gave different identities. It once stated that it was the witch of a neighbor woman named Kate Batts. This is what many people believed, and from then on, this unseen force was called "Kate" the "Bell's Witch".

It seemed that Kate had two main reasons for visiting the Bell home. The main one was to kill John Bell. For what reason no one knows because Kate never gave a reason why. The second reason was to stop John's youngest daughter Betsy from marrying a certain neighbor boy named Joshua Gardner.

On December 19, 1820, when John Bell became fell into a coma-like state.

The next morning, he died, and his family found a small bottle of fluid that they did not recognize. They gave some to one of the farm cats, which promptly died. At this point, the entity gleefully accepted responsibility for the apparent poisoning of John.

Although Bell's Witch then departed, it promised to return in 7 years. In the meantime, where had it gone?

On the Bell property lays a cave. Little is known about the cave from the historical records of the Bell's Witch. Perhaps the cave was used for storage, perhaps the children occasionally played in it as children so often do, or perhaps it was truly a gateway to hell. Perhaps the Bell's Witch had simply retreated to the cool comfort of the limestone passageways and private rooms.

Visitors to the Bell Witch Cave can make their own determinations. Some have heard voices in distant, inaccessible parts of the cave. Others have felt oppressive weights that have caused them to literally collapse to the ground. Lights and globes can be seen flitting throughout the cave and surrounding skies at night.

The original Bell farm is still a farm, but the Bell family no longer owns it, and it is not open to the public. The Bell's Witch Cave is located just off Keysburg Road in Adams, Tennessee. It is open to the public for tours by appointment only and is listed on the National Historical Registry by the United States Department of the Interior.

Likely she still languishes there, how about a visit?

Lincoln's Burial Train

Have you heard of a haunted train?

One of the most famous ghost trains of all time was Abe Lincoln's burial train, which took him home for burial in April 1865. It's also been referred to as "Lincoln's Phantom Train", and is one of the most intriguing supernatural events in American history.

After the assassination of President Abraham Lincoln, it was decided (against his wife's objections) that his body be displayed on a funeral train that would zigzag through the northern United States on its way to his home in Springfield, IL. The body was not embalmed, and a pair of funeral home employees were on hand during the whole trip to keep the deceased president looking good. They used fresh flowers to mask the smell, which meant the train needed to make frequent stops, which served to refresh the flowers and also allow mourners to pay their respects.

According to historian R.J. Norton, on the website "Abraham Lincoln's Assassination," Lincoln's funeral coach left on April 21, 1865 from the Baltimore and Ohio Depot in Washington D.C. It would run from there through to Springfield, Illinois, stopping at most major cities and many smaller ones so citizens could pay their last respects. At each stop, the President lay in state while thousands of mourners filed past the coffin.

There were so many people who wanted to view the great American leader that several additional stops had to be added along the way. By May 2, the body had become so badly discolored that the crowds were becoming upset at the sight.

On May 3, President Lincoln arrived in Springfield for the final time.

Even before the first anniversary of Lincoln's death, the first reports of the Ghost Train began to trickle into the public's collective conscience. These stories seem to have originated in the Hudson River Valley. Every year since, at the end of April during the anniversary of the first funeral trip, people all along the trains' original route report seeing an odd sight: an eerie spectral train passing silently along the tracks.

While descriptions vary, there are striking similarities in the story told. The train is easily identified by a bluish light that seems to emanate from it. Those waiting by the tracks report that the train makes no noise at all, although some witnesses have reported hearing an old-fashioned train whistle.

The ghost train, it was said, was crewed by skeletons and a similar skeleton honor guard stood watch over the casket. The sound of the train's whistle, quite different from modern locomotives, could sometimes be heard, or a puff of smoke from an invisible stack might be seen. Clocks would stop for anywhere from six minutes to twenty (the length of the actual stay). The crossing guards at the Miami Street junction also would drop mysteriously when there was nothing on the tracks.

If a real train goes by at the same time, the ghost train is replaced. A real train doesn't seem to effect the ghost train any, or vice versa.

Do the railroad tracks become haunted by Lincoln's ghost train every April since the anniversary of his last route?

Nobody knows the answer.

Amityville Horror & Spooky Franklin Castle

Amityville-

The most famous and horrific ghost story of the last century must be that of 112 Ocean Avenue, in Amityville, New York.

The terrifying tale has been turned into a best-selling book and successful film, and captured the public's attention like no other haunting. Indeed, such is its place in the American consciousness that most people assume that it is a real story – and that is certainly how it was publicized.

There is no doubt that some awful events did take place in the building, but were they really caused by ghostly actions?

The now infamous three-storey Dutch colonial house was built in 1924. The owners lived happily in the building for many years, raising a family and leaving the house to their daughter who had such fond memories of her childhood home that she moved her own family into it. In 1960 the building left the care of the original owners' descendants and was bought by a couple who lived in the house until they sold it following their divorce in 1965.

In June 1965 the DeFeo family bought the house. They were an unhappy family and the father, Ronald DeFeo Sr., was known to be abusive. Over a period of nine years the family was not said to experience any type of frightening event other than those inflicted by paternal forces. However, that all changed on the night of the 18th of November 1974 when one son, Ronald DeFeo Jr., shot and killed his mother, father, two brothers and two sisters.

Just over a year later, in December 1975, a young couple bought the house. George and Kathy Lutz, and her three children moved in, knowing the building's terrible history.

Almost immediately they began experiencing strange phenomena. Doors and windows would open by themselves, bizarre noises were heard, and a Catholic priest who had come to exorcise the house was ordered to get out by a devilish voice. Things rapidly grew worse. Blood and sticky goo oozed from the walls, clouds of flies appeared on windows, ghostly hooded apparitions manifested, and one of the children started communicating with a demonic pig called Jodie. One-night Kathy Lutz was even thrown from her bed by a supernatural force, and it was famously claimed that the face of the devil appeared in the brickwork of the fireplace.

After 28 days of this horror, the Lutzes moved out. They soon went to the media with their story.

In February 1976 two of America's most famous celebrity paranormal investigators, Ed and Lorraine Warren, were filmed by a television news team whilst conducting séances at the house.

The Warrens stated the house was indeed haunted with evil spirits, but other investigators were not convinced.

Dr Stephen Kaplan, the executive director of the Parapsychology Institute of America, based in New York, initially had great doubts about the story, and discovered some very interesting facts about the Lutzes. However, his studies were ignored, and it transpired that the couple had already collaborated with an author, Jay Anson, and had written a book, The Amityville Horror – A True Story. An instant best-seller on its release in 1977, a blockbusting movie version of the tale was released in 1979.

As Kaplan suspected, there were some dubious actions and motives behind the Amityville tale. It was revealed that Ronald DeFeo Jr's defense lawyer had met with the Lutzes before their story was released. Kaplan found no evidence to support many of the claims written in their book, but he did discover that the Lutzes were able to return to the house to hold a garage sale only a couple of weeks after apparently fleeing in terror.

Similarly, many investigators noticed that the Lutzes were holding contracts for book and film rights as soon as they decided to publicize their account. Since the Lutzes left, three different families have lived in the house with no reports of ghostly experiences. Dr Stephen Kaplan's in-depth report and its subsequent revelations about the house were never viewed with as much interest as the dramatic original story, but his book, The Amityville Horror Conspiracy, was eventually published some years after his death.

Many investigators and cynics have been led to conclude that the whole case really revolved around money, rather than the popular perception of paranormal influences. The evil forces in this story have less to do with supernatural unknowns, and more with all too common, base human instincts.

****

Franklin Castle

Franklin Castle is an eerie structure of dark and foreboding stone that has long been considered a spooky place by architects and the general public alike. There are over thirty rooms in the castle's four stories and the roof is designed in steep gables that give the place its gothic air. Secret passages honeycomb the house and sliding panels hide the doorways to these hidden corridors. It is said that a thirteen-year-old girl was once murdered in one of these hallways by her uncle because he believed her to be insane. In the front tower, it is told that a bloody ax murder once took place and it was here that one of the former owners found a secret cabinet that contained human bones. The Deputy coroner of Cleveland, Dr. Lester Adelson, who examined the bones shortly after they were found in January 1975, judged them to be of someone who had been dead for a very, very long time. Did they date back to the years of the original owners of the house?

It is hard to separate fact from fiction at Franklin Castle but we do know that a German immigrant named Hannes Tiedemann built the mansion in 1865. Tiedemann was a former barrel-maker and wholesale grocer who had gone into banking. This new source of wealth allowed him to spare no expense in building the house and he soon moved in with his wife, Luise. Over the next few years, Luise gave birth to a son, August, and a daughter, Emma but life in the mansion was never really happy. By 1881, it had become tragic.

On January 16, 15-year-old Emma died from diabetes. In those days, death from the disease came as a horrible, lingering starvation for which there was no cure. A short time later, Tiedemann's elderly mother, Wiebeka, also died in the house. Over the next three years, the Tiedemann's buried three children, one of them just eleven days old. Rumors began to spread that there may have been more to these deaths than was first apparent.

To take his wife's mind off the family tragedies, Tiedemann enlisted the services of a prominent architectural firm to design some additions to the mansion. It was during this expansion that the secret passages, concealed rooms and hidden doors were added to the house. Gas lighting was also installed throughout the building and many of the fixtures are still visible today. A large ballroom was also added that ran the length of the entire house and turrets and gargoyles were also incorporated into the design, making it appear even more like a castle.

The hidden passages in the house also hide many legends. At the rear of the house is a trap door that leads to a tunnel that goes nowhere. Another hidden room once contained a liquor still, left over from the Prohibition era. During the 1920's, the house was allegedly used as a speakeasy and warehouse for illegal liquor. The most gruesome secret uncovered in the house came from another of the hidden rooms. Here, an occupant found literally dozens of human baby skeletons. It was suggested that they may have been the victims of a doctor's botched experiments or even medical specimens, but no one knew for sure. The medical examiner simply stated that they were "old bones".

On March 24, 1895, Luise died at the age of 57 from what was said to be "liver trouble". Rumors continued to spread about the many untimely deaths in the Tiedemann family, especially when Hannes married again a few years later. By that time, he had sold the castle to a brewing family named Mullhauser and had moved to a grander home on Lake Road. The following summer, Tiedemann decided to vacation at a German resort and there he met (or some have suggested became re-acquainted with) a young waitress named Henriette. He quickly married the woman and lived just long enough to regret it. He divorced her and left her with nothing.

By 1908, Tiedemann's entire family, including his son, August and his children, had passed away. There was no one left to inherit his fortune or to comfort him in his old age. Tiedemann died later that same year, suddenly stricken while walking in the park one day. It is believed that he suffered a massive stroke.

Tiedemann's death did not end the speculation about strange events in the house however. Legend had it that Tiedemann had not been the faithful husband that he appeared to be. There were stories of affairs and sexual encounters within the vast confines of the house that were only whispered about. Tangled in the distasteful stories were also rumors of murder.

One of the bloody tales was told about a hidden passage that extended beyond the castle's ballroom. It was here that Tiedemann allegedly killed his niece by hanging her from one of the exposed rafters. The stories say that she was insane and that he killed her to put her out of her misery. But it's possible this was not the truth because others maintain that he killed her because of her promiscuity. He discovered her in bed with his grandson, it is said, and she paid the ultimate price for this transgression.

Tiedemann is also said to have murdered a young servant girl on her wedding day because she rejected his advances. Another version of the story says that the woman who was killed was Tiedemann's mistress, a woman named Rachel. She accidentally strangled to death in the house after Tiedemann tied her up and gagged her after learning that she wanted to marry another man. It's possible that Rachel's spirit is the resident "woman in black" who has been seen lurking around the old tower. Former residents say that they have heard the sound of a woman choking in this room.

More blood was spilled in the house a few years later, after the Mullhauser family sold the castle to the German Socialist Party in 1913. They used the house for meetings and parties, or so it was said. However, the legends of the house maintain that the Socialists were actually Nazi spies and that twenty of their members were machine-gunned to death in one of the castle's secret rooms. They sold the house fifty-five years later, and during the time of their residence, the house was mainly unoccupied.

It is believed that they may have rented out a portion of the house however, as a Cleveland nurse recalled several years ago that she had cared for an ailing attorney in the castle in the early 1930's. She remembered being terrified at night by the sound of a small child crying. More than forty years later, she told a reporter that she "would never set foot in that house again."

In January of 1968, James Romano, his wife, and six children moved into the house. Mrs. Romano had always been fascinated with the mansion and planned to open a restaurant there, but she quickly changed her mind. On the very day that the family moved in, she sent her children upstairs to play. A little while later, they came back downstairs and asked if they could have a cookie for their new friend, a little girl who was upstairs crying. Mrs. Romano followed the children back upstairs, but found no little girl. This happened a number of times, leading many to wonder if the "ghost children" might be the spirits of the Tiedemann children who died in the early 1880's.

Mrs. Romano also reported hearing organ music in the house, even though no organ was there and sounds of footsteps tramping up and down the hallways. She also heard voices and the sound of glass clinking on the third floor, even though no one else was in the house. The Romano's finally consulted a Catholic priest about the house. He declined to do an exorcism of the place, but told them that he sensed an evil presence in the house and that they should leave.

The family then turned to the Northeast Ohio Psychical Research Society, a now defunct ghost-hunting group, and they sent out a team to investigate Franklin Castle. In the middle of the investigation, one of the team members fled the building in terror.

By September of 1974, the Romano's had finally had enough. They sold the castle to Sam Muscatello, who planned to turn the place into a church, but instead, after learning of the building's shady past, started offering guided tours of the house. He also had problems with ghostly visitors in the mansion encountering strange sounds, vanishing objects and the eerie woman in black.

He invited Cleveland radio executive John Webster to the house for an on-air special about hauntings and Franklin Castle. Webster claimed that while walking up a staircase, something tore a tape recorder from a strap over his shoulder and flung it down the stairs. "I was climbing the stairs with a large tape recorder strapped over my shoulder," Webster later recalled and then told how the device was pulled away from him. "I just stood there holding the microphone as I watched the tape recorder go flying down to the bottom of the stairs, where it broke into pieces."

A television reporter named Ted Ocepec, who also came to visit the castle, witnessed a hanging ceiling light that suddenly began turning in circular motions. He was also convinced that something supernatural lurked in the house. Someone suggested that perhaps traffic vibrations on the street outside had caused the movement of the light. Ocepec didn't think so. "I just don't know," he said, "but there's something in that house."

Muscatello's interest in the history of the house led him to start searching for the secret panels and passages installed by the Tiedemann's. It was he who made the gruesome discovery of the skeleton behind the panel in the tower room. This discovery apparently had a strange effect on Muscatello as he started becoming sick and lost over thirty pounds in a few weeks. He was never very successful at turning the place into a tourist attraction and eventually sold the place to a doctor, who in turn sold the house for the same amount to Cleveland Police Chief Richard Hongisto.

The police chief and his wife declared that the spacious mansion would make the perfect place in which to live but then, less than one year later, abruptly sold the house to George Mirceta, who was unaware of the house's haunted reputation. He had bought the castle merely for its solid construction and Gothic architecture. He lived alone in the house and also conducted tours of the place, asking visitors to record any of their strange experiences in a guest book before leaving. Some reported seeing a woman in white, babies crying and lights swinging back and forth. One woman even complained of feeling like she was being choked in the tower room. Strangely, she had no idea of the legend concerning that room and the death of Tiedemann's mistress.

Even though he had a number of strange experiences while living there, Mirceta maintained that the castle was not haunted. If it was, he told reporters, he would be too scared to live there. "There has to be a logical explanation for everything," he told an interviewer.

In 1984, the house was sold once again, this time to Michael De Vinko, who attempted to restore the place. He claimed to have no problems with ghosts in the house but surmised that it may have been because he was taking care of the old place again. He spent huge sums of money in restoration efforts. He successfully tracked down the original blueprints to the house, some of the Tiedemann furniture, and even the original key to the front door, which still worked. Even after spending all of the money though, the house was put back on the real-estate market in 1994.

The castle was sold again in 1999 and the new owner once again attempted to restore the place, even after an arson fire damaged it badly in November of that same year. Work continued throughout his ownership, as he hoped to open the place once again for tours. But had the blood-soaked past of the house left a mark that was still being felt in the present? When asked if the castle was really haunted, the owner admitted that he was not sure that it was, or if he even believed in ghosts at all. However, he did say that many of his friends and family have had had odd experiences here. "Most of them involve either unexplained sounds, or difficult-to-describe feelings."

He added that the castle was not a scary place, but it was a little creepy, especially in the middle of the night. "I've heard strange sounds and hoped to see something or hear something that would prove to me that ghosts exist, but so far it hasn't happened," he said. "So far it's been no spookier than sleeping alone in any old house that creaks in the wind or has rattling pipes." It was sold again in 2004.

Most recently, Cuyahoga County real estate records show the castle and rear carriage house sold in late August 2011 for $260,000 to "Oh Dear! Productions LLC." Oh Dear! Productions is registered as a Foreign Limited Liability Company with the Ohio Secretary of State. Oh Dear! Productions LLC was organized in the state of Delaware in August, 2011.

Today, Franklin Castle has a new owner who says he will be restoring the mansion to its original glory and using it as a residence. Let's see, how long will he last in this spooky castle.

PUZZLING PEOPLE

- *Dracula*

- *Kaspar Hauser*

- *Queen of Sheba*

- *King Arthur*

- *Giacomo Girolamo Casanova*

- *Donnie Decker, The Rain Boy*

- *The Isdal Woman*

- *Robin Hood*

- *The Green Children of Woolpit*

- *Gil Pérez- Teleportation from Philippines To Mexico*

- *The Man in The Iron Mask*

- *Scary Shadow People-*

- *Db Cooper*

- *Dr Barry's Deathbed S*X Secret-*

- *The Strange Case of Rudolph Fentz*

Dracula:

Eastern Europe of the Middle Ages was a turbulent place. The great Hungarian nation was its first line of defense against Ottoman forces, and the individual states that happened to be placed in 'No-man's land' between the two suffered terrible unrest.

It was enough to inspire Bram Stoker to write his most famous novel, although people now question which figure during this unstable period was the greatest influence on the writer. Only one name truly stands out – the real, terrible man known as Dracula.

Walachia, now part of Romania, was a Hungarian province ruled by Prince Mircea the Old until 1418. In around 1390, Mircea had an illegitimate son named Vlad who was given away to be brought up in the court of Hungary's King Sigismund. When Mircea died, Vlad was not given control of Walachia, but he was made a Knight of the Order of the Dragon, a group set up to defend the Christian world from Turkish rule.

Vlad was soon given the name 'Dracul', meaning 'dragon', and was made governor of Transylvania. Dracul had three sons. The first, named after his father Mircea, was born in 1443, with the next two called Vlad and Radu. Dracul gathered an army and took back his family's traditional seat of power in Walachia, although only with the help of old enemy Turkey. As a sign of his loyalty, Dracul sent Vlad and Radu to live in Adrianople, the seat of the Ottoman Empire.

In 1447 Dracul and Mircea were killed, and a Hungarian government again ruled Walachia. This situation made

Turkey uncomfortable, so in 1448 they decided to arm the seventeen-year-old Vlad who was known as the 'Son of Dragon', or Dracula. Over the years and battles the protagonists continued to swap sides, but by 1456 Dracula had reclaimed his throne in Walachia. He built a capital city at Tirgoviste and was pronounced Prince Vlad III. From the beginning, he realized that to survive he would have to be shown as utterly ruthless. Shortly after he was crowned prince, he invited destitute souls from the streets of his kingdom to a great feast at his castle. After the meal, he asked the assembled poor, frail and aged if they would 'like to be without cares, lacking nothing in the world?' When they all cried 'yes' he promptly boarded up the castle and set fire to it. He said there was little place in his society for people who would be a burden, and anybody who did not contribute to the community received scant sympathy.

If killing the infirm was a sign to the public, Dracula committed a similar action with Walachia's dignitaries. He had the older ones impaled, and sent the others to build a castle at Poenari, a mountainous area 50 miles away.

In their place, Dracula organized his own set of nobles to confirm his power. His evil knew no bounds, and he particularly enjoyed watching people die after being hoisted on a sharpened pole. His people called him Vlad Tepes meaning 'Vlad the Impaler' and the Turkish knew him as Kaziglu Bey or the 'Impaler Prince'. He murdered cheating wives, fraudulent merchants, anybody who committed any crime. Often, he would have many victims impaled at the same time, but he also enjoyed skinning and boiling people alive. He killed children and the old, and put their bodies on public display to warn would-be miscreants. It is said that 20,000 dead bodies hung from the walls of Tirgoviste, and by the end of his reign he had killed around 50,000 people. In 1462 when Walachia was attacked by the Turks, led by

Dracula's younger brother Radu, Dracula went into exile in Hungary.

In 1476, with Radu dead of syphilis and another prince on Walachia's throne, Dracula attempted to regain his rightful home. He succeeded, but in December 1476 was killed during another Turkish attack. The Ottoman sultan impaled Dracula's head and had it displayed in Constantinople as evidence of his death. His body was said to have been buried as an island monastery called Snagov, although investigative digs in 1931 were unable to find the coffin. It is one final mystery to the Dracula story. Some proof of his reign does remain though.

His fortress in the hills of Poenari stands today as a popular tourist destination, and there are also ruins of his palace at Tirgoviste,

Kaspar Hauser

On May 26, 1828 (Easter Monday), two men were talking together in the Unschlittsplatz near Nuremberg's New Gate when they were approached by a teenage boy. By all accounts, he was a fresh-complexioned boy of about seventeen years of age and dressed like a peasant. Although remarkably short for his age, there was nothing else notable about him except for his dusty clothing and general appearance of having walked a long way.

After asking for directions to New Gate Street, he pulled a letter out of his pocket addressed to "The Captain of the Fourth Squadron of the Schmollischer Regiment, Neue Thor Strasse (New Gate Street), Nuremberg". One of the men, a shoemaker named Weichmann, offered to take the boy there as he was heading in that direction. Along the way, they chatted briefly and Weichman assumed he was just a stable boy based on the Low Bavarian dialect that he used to speak. After introducing the boy to a regimental corporal, Weichmann went on his way.

The captain, opened the letter. It explained that the boy had been left with a poor laborer who had kept him locked inside all his life. But the boy was now ready to serve in the king's army. The cavalry captain questioned the boy, but the only words he said were, 'don't know', 'take me home', and 'horse'.

He could also write the name 'Kaspar Hauser'.

In the end, the captain put the boy in the local prison but the jailer took pity on him. The jailer's children began to teach him to speak, write and draw. He seemed to have no concept of behavior; had no facial expressions; could not understand the difference between men and women; was happy to sleep sitting up; acted like a baby or infant child and was particularly happy in the dark.

In July 1828 a local magistrate suggested to Nuremberg's authorities that it would be best for Hauser to be taken out of the jail and placed in the custody of George Friedrich Daumer, a university professor and psychologist.

Daumer helped Hauser change into a normal young man, but also kept a record of the strange boy's behaviour. Daumer realized the extent of Hauser's amazing heightened senses. He could read in the dark, hear whispers from extreme distances and discern who was in a pitch-black room simply by their smell.

Unfortunately, as his awareness and education about the world around him increased, these extraordinary abilities waned.

By early 1829, Hauser had learnt enough to be able to write his autobiography. In it he revealed that he had been kept in a cell 7ft long, 4ft wide and 5ft high by a man whose face he never saw. He slept on a straw bed, and when he woke there would be water and bread for him to eat. Sometimes the water would taste odd, and he would pass out only to find himself cleaned and groomed, wearing with a fresh set of clothes when he awoke.

One day the man came to Hauser's cell door with books and taught him to read a little, write his name, and repeat the rudimentary phrases he pronounced on his public arrival. The next day, Hauser and his captor began a three-day journey which culminated in his appearance at Nuremberg. Hauser's autobiography opened the door to a new terror.

In October 1829 a stranger dressed in black came to

Daumer's house and tried to kill Hauser with a knife. Lord Stanhope, an English aristocrat and friend of the ruling Baden family, then struck up a friendship with Hauser, and gained guardianship of the boy from the city of Nuremberg. Stanhope quickly lost interest and placed the boy in the town of Ansbach under the care of a Dr Meyer. Meyer disliked the boy and became a hard and mean-spirited tutor.

On 14th December 1831, Hauser went to a local park to meet a man who had promised to reveal details about his mother's identity. They met, and the stranger motioned as if to give Hauser a wallet, but as the young man leant forward, he was stabbed in his side. He died three days later aged just 21.

The suspicion developed that Hauser was actually a Baden prince and son of Stephanie, Grand Duchess of Bavaria. Certainly, many of the Bavarian aristocracy had such suspicions, and King Ludwig of Bavaria even wrote in his diary that Hauser was the 'rightful Grand Duke of Baden'.

The theory is that Stephanie and Karl of Baden had Hauser in 1812, but Karl's stepmother, the Duchess of Hochberg, switched him at birth with a sickly peasant child. The ill baby soon passed away and subsequent boys sired by Karl with Stephanie also died young. Karl himself died in strange circumstances, and on his deathbed said he believed that he and his boys had been poisoned. Karl's throne then went to his stepbrother, the Duchess of Hochberg's son Leopold. It is an unprovable theory.

All we definitely know is that in a peaceful countryside churchyard there is a gravestone that reads:

'Here lies Kaspar Hauser, riddle of his time.

His birth was unknown, his death mysterious.

Queen of Sheba

Queen of Sheba is recorded in the First Book of Kings in the Old Testament. It states that around the tenth century BC a queen of the rich trading nation known as Sheba decided to meet the great King Solomon in person.

She did not believe the stories she had been told of Solomon's wisdom, and brought many hard questions to test him. When his replies met with her approval, she gave him plentiful gifts of gold, spices and precious stones. In return, Solomon gave the queen 'all her desire', and after their meeting she returned to her own country. The story is repeated in the second Book of Chronicles, and even Christ himself spoke of a queen of the south who came to hear the wisdom of Solomon.

Other than this, precious few pieces of historical evidence have survived, but that has not stopped the growth of countless myths and stories.

So, who was the real Queen of Sheba?

Perhaps the most famous and important extension of her story is that connected with Ethiopia.

In 1320 an Ethiopian monk named Yetshak wrote a compendium of legends called Kebra Negast or 'Glory of the Kings'. In it, he said that when the Queen of Sheba, referred to in Ethiopian as Makeda, visited Solomon, she was seduced by the great king. Solomon had said that the queen was welcome to his hospitality, but must not take anything without asking. During the night, the Queen suffered a terrible thirst caused by a spicy meal Solomon fed her and she drank the water placed by her bed. The king said she had broken the rules, and must sleep with him as repayment. Nine months later she gave birth to a boy called Menelik. Ethiopians believe that the Queen and her son both accepted the Jewish faith, and that Menelik founded the Solomon Jewish, and then Christian, dynasty in Aksum, Ethiopia. At around the same time as Yetshak was compiling his tome, other legends were forming in Europe.

A thirteenth century story told in the Legenda Aurea stated that the queen was a prophetess connected to the crucifixion of Christ. Over time, she also became an integral part of religious decorations and art. She was often seen as a sorceress, and then a seductress.

Strangely, she is also featured as having a secret deformity – French Gothic sculpture often shows her having a webbed foot.

In the same way, the Temptation of Saint Anthony by French novelist Gustave Flaubert depicts the queen as a lustful temptress with a withered limb. This imperfection perhaps arises from earlier Jewish and Islamic references to her.

In both the Koran and the Jewish Book called the Targum Sheni, the queen meets Solomon and reveals that she has hairy feet. The Jewish tradition later features her as a demon or seductress, whereas Islamic legend states that Solomon used his magicians' power to remove her excess hair and married her. Muslims call the Queen of Sheba Balkis, and believe her great nation was based in the Yemen.

The Koran describes Sheba as being two gardens, irrigated by a great dam. An advanced level of farming, and good access to Red Sea shipping channels and Arabian camel trains, meant the nation prospered.

Archaeological proof of this occurring in Southern Arabia has been uncovered. The remains of a great dam can be viewed in the Mareb region of the Yemen, now considered to be the capital of the ancient Sheba nation.This dam collapsed in AD 543, but scientists have been able to deduce that it would have been used to irrigate over 500 acres of farm land.

In recent years, archaeologists have finished restoring an ancient temple known as the 'Throne of Balkis' in the Mareb region. The structure dates from the tenth century BC, so is from the right era to link with what we do know about the queen.

Two miles to the east of the Marab region, another ancient building, known as the 'Temple of the Moon God', is also being studied.

Scientists using radar equipment believe this is an extremely large and elaborate structure, and could yield the answers to many Sheba mysteries.

Unfortunately, such investigations have been plagued over the years by political indifference and, until these areas become more secure for researchers to study, the true history of Sheba may continue to be obscured by myth and legend.

King Arthur

The legend of King Arthur states that he was born sometime in the fifth century AD. It is said that the great magician Merlin disguised Uther Pendragon, one of Britain's great warriors, to look like the Duke of Tintagel, the husband of Ingraine of Cornwall.

Uther seduced Ingraine at Tintagel cottage, but the child they conceived was given away at birth. He was named Arthur and was raised completely unaware of his special lineage. When Uther died, the throne was empty. Merlin set a sword called Excalibur in rock and stated that only someone of a truly royal bloodline would be able to remove Excalibur from its fixed position.

When the young Arthur was the only one able to do this, he was pronounced king. Eleven other British rulers rebelled against the young leader, but Arthur quashed their uprising and began a noble and glorious reign. Arthur married Guinevere and assembled a group of courageous and honest knights at a kingdom seat in Camelot, in the Vale of Avalon. To avoid any sense of preference among the knights, Guinevere's father provided Arthur with the fabled Round Table. Together they had great victories over Saxon invaders and the Roman Empire.

Arthur is even said to have become Emperor himself and set about on a search for the Holy Grail.

However, during this time one of Arthur's most trusted knights, Lancelot, had an affair with Guinevere. This marked the beginning of the end for Arthur. The two lovers fled to Lancelot's land in Brittany, France. Arthur decided to follow and wage war on his former friend, leaving his nephew Mordred as custodian of England. Whilst he was battling across the English Channel, Mordred rebelled, so Arthur was forced to return home. A fierce battle ensued on Salisbury Plain. Arthur managed to kill Mordred, but the king himself was also mortally wounded.

On the brink of death, he returned to Avalon. He is said to have thrown Excalibur into that kingdom's lake and then he himself disappeared into a cave, pledging he would return if ever danger threatened England.

The first historical proof we have of an Arthurian-type figure is in Gildas' sixth century De Excidio Britanniae which refers to British soldiers being led by a man called Ambrosius Aurelianus. The name 'Arthur' appears in Nennius' ninth century Historia Brittonum.

However, it was not until the twelfth century that the phenomenon of Arthur as an historical icon really had an impact. William of Malmesbury and Geoffrey of Monmouth produced works which sowed the seeds of our modern understanding of Athurian legend.

Unfortunately, their works also included many fictional details, which have subsequently obscured the true reality of Arthur's reign.

There is other evidence for his place in historical fact. Many people believe that Glastonbury in Somerset is the true site of Camelot, and in the 12th century it was claimed that Arthur's grave had been found there.

Similarly, the Isles of Scilly are said to host the remains of the great king.

Certainly, there are plenty of candidates for places featured in Arthurian mythology and historians have discovered many possible historical figures who could be the king himself.

The historians believe that the sheer number of possibilities as to Arthur's true identity is probably the reason that our knowledge has become so blurred, and that many individual personal histories have been actually confused and amalgamated.

What we do know is that in the sixth century many Celtic realms had leaders born who were called Arthur; this could have been in homage to the original king. Although the use of the name has clouded the original Arthur's legend, it also points to the fact that a truly great and inspirational leader was present a generation before.

Perhaps that most amazing evidence has only surfaced in recent years. In July 1998, archaeologists found a slab marked in Latin with the name 'Artagnov' or 'Arthnou' on a rocky hilltop in Tintagel, Cornwall. The slab dates to the sixth century, and proves that the name was present in the legendary Arthurian lands at the correct time, and belonged to a man of some standing.

Like many historical mysteries, the damage to truth caused by passing years, is slowly being fixed by science and the application of modern interest. We may never know exactly who the legend of King Arthur represents, but with more finds like this, we can only move closer to the tantalizing truth.

Giacomo Girolamo Casanova

Giacomo Girolamo Casanova (April 2, 1725 – June 4, 1798) was a Venetian adventurer and author. His main book History de ma vies (Story of My Life), part autobiography and part memoir, is regarded as one of the most authentic sources of the customs and norms of European social life during the 18th century. So famous a womanizer was he that his name remains synonymous with the art of seduction and he is sometimes called "the world's greatest lover". He enjoyed the company of European royalty, popes and cardinals, along with men such as Voltire, Goethe and Mozart; but if he had not been obliged to spend some years as a librarian in the household of Count Waldstein of Bohemia (where he relieved his boredom by writing the story of his life), he would probably be forgotten today.

Jacques Casanova de Seingalt as he called himself in his memoirs was tall, good looking with bright dark eyes and a beaked nose. He was, you might say, the Valentino of his day.

He seduced amorous nuns, virgins (some as young as 13), innumerable married women, two sisters at the same time, a castrato ("he" turned out to be a "she"), he traveled with a lesbian companion, he escaped from the dreaded Leads prison in Venice and he displayed great skill in the magic arts.

His passion for women was only an extension of his amazing passion for life, living and people. It didn't hurt either that he was a prodigy, a polymath, brilliant in almost every subject and fluent in five different languages. He made and lost half a dozen fortunes, lived in every major European city before it was fashionable nor reasonable, hung out with

Kings (Frederick the Great, Catherine the Great, Louis XV), intellectuals (Voltaire, Rousseau), and artists (Mozart). He also hung out with monks and beggars. He survived the Inquisition, escaped from prison, wrote over 40 books and was banished from three different countries.

His legacy is beyond women — it's that of living life to it's most possible limits, disregarding the ideas of "success" or "failure" in favor of simply having experiences and appreciating them. As he said in his memoirs, "Whether you think my actions good or bad, no one can deny, that I truly lived."

He wrote about sexual experiences with 133 women in his memoirs. He notes that he purposely left out a dozen or so who's reputation he didn't want to tarnish (probably very famous women). He stopped his memoirs when he turned 42.

If Casanova was a romantic it was because he had the good fortune to have experienced true love once in his life, even though he knew it was transitory. The woman in question was Henriette, a beautiful young woman whom he met in his younger days. Her role switching resembles Casanova's own and perhaps they were both French spies at one time. If she too was a romantic, then she understood the limits of romantic love -- after three great months together she left him. She wanted to marry a husband who would remain constant in his sexual attentions and his finances, just as she knew she herself would not remain constant. If Casanova was her true love then she knew equally that he could never be constant either. They were equals. For such lovers the truest form of love is a fantasy you carry throughout your life for your perfect sexual mate that can only be diminished by staying together. Such a love is a Romantic notion.

There was a dramatic surge of interest in the 1920s when a

ton of books about Casanova appeared and further translations followed, but with all the risqué bits still cut out. For Casanova this only confirmed that the present was not the revenge of the past upon the present but the revenge of the present upon the past. Civilization did not progress; it regressed. In 1797, word arrived that the Republic of Venice had ceased to exist and Napoleon Bonaparte had seized Casanova's home city. It was too late to return home. Casanova died on June 4, 1798, at age 73. His last words are said to have been "I have lived as a philosopher and I die as a Christian"

It is said, the grumpy old ghost of Casanova still haunts the library of the Castle of Dux (where he was the librarian to Count Joseph Karl von Waldstein, a chamberlain of the emperor, in the Castle of Dux, Bohemia (Duchcov Castle, Czech Republic)). The Castle squats in western Bohemia, passing through time like a ship passes through space, the clouds soaring overhead. The ghost has been at war for many years with the vicious little mediocrities employed at the Castle who barge in from time to time to fling insults at him. He has rigged a trap over the door into the library and next time, he plans to flatten them with an avalanche of his heaviest German philosophy books.

Casanova had found that as he got older the criticism intensified as if old men were not allowed to seduce younger women occasionally. Did this mean a tragic decline into dotage? No. He did not have to be turned into a symbol overloaded with unnatural meanings.

Though having had hundreds of lovers, over a dozen marriage proposals, eight illegitimate children, and thousands of friends and acquaintances — many in high places — he died miserable, bitter, and alone.

Donnie Decker, the Rain Boy

Donnie Decker of Stroudsburg, Pennsylvania, had a troubled young adulthood. Imprisoned whilst still an adolescent there was little in his life he could boast of. But what he could boast of was scarily impressive - He could make it rain - ANYWHERE. Whether it was indoors or out, Donnie could summon rain from the sky, roofs, ceilings, floors, you name it, Donnie could flood it. In order to pay his last respects and attend the funeral of his Grandfather, Donnie was released from prison where he was serving a 12-month sentence for receiving stolen goods.

Unknown to everyone within the family, Donnie had been carrying a secret about his Grandfather since the age of 7 years old. Donnie Decker alleges that his Grandfather had been repeatedly physically abusing him. Who knows what emotional turmoil that unleashes within the mind and spirit of an adolescent but there are those in authority who say Donnie Decker made it manifest in a series of puzzling paranormal events.

Donnie was disturbed by the reverence shown to his Grandfather at the funeral and afterwards, spending the night with friends, the Keefer's, those feelings erupted in a way that could never have been foreseen. As he sat quietly with his friends suddenly the air around him turned cold, and at the same time, water started to drip from the living-room walls. Donnie fell into a strange trance like state. The tenants of the property immediately called the landlord, Ron H. Van Why to report that water was now dripping from the walls and the ceiling.

When Ron arrived, he was mystified as seeing what was happening. As the landlord he knew where the plumbing pipes were located and there were none anywhere near the vicinity of the room. The plumbing was all at the rear of the building and the water was pouring through one room only where no pipes were located. Ron quickly realized that water wasn't simply travelling downwards from the walls and ceiling - it was pouring up out of the floor too. At this point he called in the local Police.

Patrolman John Baujan couldn't believe his eyes and was taken aback enough by what was unfolding before him to call in his partner Patrolman Richard Wolbert. Together they stepped into the one room which was affected by the water and immediately both were drenched through. Scarily, both watched as droplets of water travelled horizontally between them and travelled out of the room in midair.

Police advised that the family and Donnie leave the premises and go to a nearby cafe while they investigated, but Ron (who had also brought along his wife), elected to stay. As the Keefer's and Donnie Decker left the building, suddenly the water stopped pouring. Ron surmised that somehow one of them was responsible for causing the 'indoor rain' - but which one?

It had now been almost a full 24 hours since the indoor rain started and as they sat in the local cafe Donnie still appeared 'trance like' - Cafe owner Pam Scarfano who had earlier witnessed the rain in the house thought out loud that maybe Donnie was responsible and that maybe it was the 'Devil's work'? 'Maybe he was possessed'?

No sooner had Pam, the Keefers and Donnie seated themselves around a cafe table than the seemingly impossible happened - it started to rain inside the cafe. Alarmed Pam rushed to her cash register where she kept a crucifix and placed it around Donnie's neck - it immediately turned black but burned Donnie on the neck leaving visible markings upon him. The Keefers and Donnie decided to leave the cafe and as they did so once again the 'rain' stopped. It was at this point the concensus appeared to be that Donnie was responsible for causing it to happen. Back at the house the rain had started again and accusations towards Donnie started to fly. At this stage the pots and pans on the stove started to rattle and without warning Donnie suddenly levitated and was thrown across the room. The Police Chief was called in and given the time of evening was annoyed at being called out - he put the whole thing down to 'plumbing issues' and ordered his men to leave - Unusually, he also ordered his men to say nothing of the incident and not to file a report.

The following day Lieutenant William Davies of the local Police Force became yet another authoritative witness to the events in the house. He and Lieutenant John Rundle then witnessed the seemingly impossible happen again - Once again Donnie Decker was levitated off the floor and hurled across the room. When they rushed to his aid, they found three claw marks upon his neck. It is worth bearing in mind at this point that we now have four experienced, respected and completely trustworthy officers of the law who have witnessed the seemingly impossible happen.

Three nights later the rain was still pouring down inside the house with the Police still drawing a blank on what could be causing it. An exorcism for Donnie seemed the only possible answer - but every Catholic and Protestant Priest or Minister turned police, friends and the landlords request down. Eventually an Evangelical preacher was found who agreed to perform the exorcism. Although Donnie convulsed during the ritual, things appeared to calm down and the rain stopped. The results however were temporary.

Returning to prison after his compassionate leave was over, Donnie was placed in a maximum-security cell and once again the 'rain' started. Startled guards removed Donnie from his soaking wet cell and accused him of throwing water from the sink around his cell. Donnie not only knew differently, but felt differently about this strange ability now however.

As he pointed out to the guards 'I can make it happen anywhere, and I can control it'. The guards then taunted him with the challenge of making it rain somewhere like the Warden's Office. Lieutenant David Keenhold was acting warden and sitting in his office oblivious to the events going on with Donnie when a guard came into the office to explain what was happening - upon standing up the warden only then became aware that his shirt was saturated with water. He hadn't felt it happen to him as he had been focused on writing a report. When the guard explained that Donnie had said he would make it rain in the warden's office the warden was mystified and in his own testimony states that he and the guard were both scared at what was going on.

The Warden called in a local Reverend, the Reverend William Blackburn. The Reverend accused Donnie of making things up and a rattled Donnie replied by raising his fingers and making it rain right there, right then. Shocked the Reverend realized Donnie did have the power to make it rain and reached the immediate conclusion that he was possessed. Performing some religious rites, the Reverend appears to have dispelled the ability Donnie had. Since then it's an ability Donnie has never been able to recreate.

Eventually, he was released from jail and found a job as a cook at a local restaurant. His present whereabouts is unknown – as is the cause of the mysterious rain.

Was it a hoax or yet another baffling mystery, no one knows.

The Isdal Woman

The Isdal woman (Norwegian: Isdalskvinnen) is the subject of an unsolved case involving an unidentified woman found dead at Isdalen Valley in Bergen, Norway on 29 November 1970.

Considered one of Norway's most profound mysteries, the case has been the subject of intense speculation over the years regarding the identity of the victim, the events leading up to her death and the cause of death.

Public interest in the case remains significant.

The woman was found in a part of Isdalen popularly known as "Death Valley", which lies in the direction towards Mount Ulriken.

Next to the scene police found a burned-out passport. The autopsy showed that the woman had suffered blunt force trauma to the neck and had taken several sleeping pills before she died.

The official police report concluded suicide, but this conclusion is highly controversial. Police traced the woman to two suitcases that were found in an NSB train station in Bergen.

Police also found that the labels had been removed from every piece of clothing she wore, and that her fingerprints had been sanded away.

Police eventually found out that the woman had travelled around Norway and Europe with nine different identities:

Jenevive Lancia, Claudia Tjelt, Vera Schlosseneck, Claudia Nielsen, Alexia Zarna-Merchez, Vera Jarle, Finella Lorck and Elizabeth Leen Hoywfer.

All of these identities were false. According to witness sightings the woman used various wigs, and in the trunk, there were found several cryptic diary entries.

Witnesses reported that the woman had spoken several languages: French, German, English and Flemish. On 24 November, five days before the discovery of the woman, a local 26-year old man was hiking with friends around the same area.

He reported to have come across a woman of foreign appearance, her face completely distorted by fear.

He noted that the woman was dressed elegantly, although not appropriately for being outdoors, let alone hiking in the hills. As they passed each other she formed her mouth as if to say something but appeared intimidated by two black-coated men who followed her.

A murder unsolved, the question is, was she a spy? If yes, then what was her purpose.

Robin Hood

Literary references of Robin Hood -- beloved today as a vigilante outlaw and rebellious philanthropist -- stretch back to at least the 13th- 14th century. Retold in countless variations, Robin Hood's resume has been expanded and enriched extensively during the intervening centuries. Poets, playwrights and directors have all seized on the good outlaw theme and run with it, breathing new life into the legend again and again. This in turn has led many researchers to sort through the annals of the past, attempting to uncover the man behind the myth, the real Robin Hood who inspired such a devoted following.

But history is as murky as a forest blanketed in predawn fog. Discerning the truth through hundreds of years of repetitive studies and speculations is like trying to hit a target with an arrow while blindfolded. Plus, any pertinent facts and public records, ones that could determine the verdict once and for all, likely either no longer exist or possibly never existed in the first place.

Origin-

Robin Hood was the legendary bandit of England who stole from the rich to help the poor. The stories about Robin appealed to common folk because he stood up against — and frequently outwitted — people in power. Furthermore, his life in the forest — hunting and feasting with his fellow outlaws, coming to the assistance of those in need — seemed like a great and noble adventure.

Early Sources-

The earliest known mention of Robin Hood is in William Langland's 1377 work called Piers Plowman, in which a character mentions that he knows "rimes of Robin Hood." This and other references from the late 1300s suggest that Robin Hood was well established as a popular legend by that time.

One source of that legend may lie in the old French custom of celebrating May Day. A character called Robin des Bois, or Robin of the Woods, was associated with this spring festival and may have been transplanted to England—with a slight name change. May Day celebrations in England in the 1400s featured a festival "king" called Robin Hood.

Also, a collection of ballads about the outlaw Robin Hood, A Lytell Geste of Robin Hode, was published in England around 1489.

Later Versions-

By the 1500s, more elaborate versions of the legend had begun to appear. Some of these suggested that Robin was a nobleman who had fallen into disgrace and had taken to the woods to live with other outlaws. Robin also acquired a girlfriend named Maid Marian and a new companion; a monk called Friar Tuck. His adventures were then definitely linked to Sherwood Forest.

Beginning in the 1700s, various scholars attempted to link Robin Hood with a real-life figure—either a nobleman or an outlaw. But none of their theories have stood up to close examination. Robin was most likely an imaginary creation, although some of the tales may have been associated with a real outlaw.

Also, at about this time, Robin began to be linked with the reigns of King Richard I, "The Lionhearted," who died in 1189, and of King John, who died in 1216. The original medieval ballads, however, contain no references to these kings or to a particular time in which Robin was supposed to have lived.

Later versions of the Robin Hood legend placed more emphasis on Robin's nobility and on his romance with Marian than on the cruelty and social tension that appear in the early ballads. In addition to inspiring many books and poems over the centuries, Robin Hood became the subject of several operas and, in modern times, numerous movies.

Tales of Robin Hood-

One of the medieval ballads about Robin Hood involved Sir Guy of Gisborne. Robin and his comrade Little John had an argument and parted. While Little John was on his own, the Sheriff of Nottingham captured him and tied him to a tree. Robin ran into Sir Guy, who had sworn to slay the outlaw leader. When they each discovered the other's identity, they drew their swords and fought. Robin killed Sir Guy and put on his clothes.

Disguised as Sir Guy, Robin persuaded the sheriff to let him kill Little John, who was still tied to the tree. However, instead of slaying Little John, Robin freed him, and the two outlaws drove off the sheriff's men.

Another old story, known as Robin Hood and the Monk, also began with a quarrel between Robin and John. Robin went into Nottingham to attend church, but a monk recognized him and raised the alarm. Robin killed 12 people before he was captured.

When word of his capture reached Robin's comrades in the forest, they planned a rescue. As the monk passed by on his way to tell the king of Robin's capture, Little John and Much seized and beheaded him. John and Much, in disguise, visited the king in London and then returned to Nottingham bearing documents sealed with the royal seal. The sheriff, not recognizing them, welcomed the two men and treated them to a feast. That night Little John and Much killed Robin's jailer and set Robin free. By the time the sheriff realized what had happened, the three outlaws were safe in Sherwood Forest.

Robin Hood's role as the enemy of the people who held power and the protector of the poor was clearly illustrated in lines from 'A Lytell Geste of Robin Hode'. Robin instructed his followers to do no harm to farmers or countrymen, but to "beat and bind" the bishops and archbishops and never to forget the chief villain, the high sheriff of Nottingham. Some ballads ended with the sheriff's death; in others, the outlaws merely embarrassed the sheriff and stole his riches. In one ballad, the sheriff was robbed and then forced to dress in outlaw green and dine with Robin and his comrades in the forest.

The Death of Robin Hood

Legend says that Robin Hood was wounded in a fight and fled to a convent. The head of the nuns there was his cousin, and he begged her for help. She made a cut so that blood could flow from his vein, a common medical practice of the time. Unknown to Robin, however, she was his enemy. She left him without tying up the vein, and he lay bleeding in a locked room. Severely weakened, he sounded three faint blasts on his horn. His friends in the forest heard his cry for help and came to the convent, but they were too late to save Robin. He shot one last arrow, and they buried him where it landed.

Over time, the image of Robin as a clever, lighthearted prankster gained strength. The tales in which he appeared as a highway robber and murderer were forgotten or rewritten.

But is he real?

While some historians claim Robin Hood is based on an actual historical person, most remain skeptical.

Verifiable hard facts haven't been uncovered, so claims are based solely on peripheral data and interpretations of the earliest known surviving works that allude to him.

These medieval literary pieces include the first passing mention of the hero in William Langland's "Piers Plowman" circa 1377, as well as the first lengthy incarnation, a ballad whose title now ranges from "A Lytyll Geste of Robyn Hode" all the way to the "Gest of Robin Hood," encompassing nearly every possible spelling in between.

A trio of three other ballads round out the ranks of the early works: "Robin Hood and the Monk," "Robin Hood and the Potter" and "Robin Hood and Guy of Gisborne."

Candidates-

Robert fitz Ooth - Earl of Huntingdon

Born 1160 - Died 1247

In 1746, Dr. William Stukeley put forward the theory that the true identity of Robin Hood was Robert fitz Odo (or Fitzooth). According to Stukeley, he was born at Loxley and lived for 87 years. Robert fitz ooth was outlawed in the 12th.

Robert de Kyme

Born c1210 - Died c1285

The eldest son of William de Kyme, Robert de Kyme was of Saxon blood. He was outlawed in 1226 for robbery and disturbing the King's peace and pardoned in 1227. According to Nottingham author Jim Lees, events in de Kyme's life bear a resemblance to events in the "Little Geste" ballad including his return to the forest as an outlaw following his pardon.

Robin Hood of the Wakefield Rolls

Born 1290 - Died 1347

In 1852, Joseph Hunter's examination of historical documents led to the postulation that Robin Hood was actually Robert Hood who appeared in the Wakefield Court Rolls in 1316 and 1317. According to this theory, Robert Hood became an outlaw not through theft but through his support for Thomas, Earl of Lancaster who rebelled against King Edward 11 at the battle of Boroughbridge in 1322. Robert Hood was born at Loxley near Sheffield and, at the age of fifteen, killed his stepfather with a scythe during an argument. He fled to Barnsdale and then on to Wakefield where he appears in court roll entries for a string of minor offences.

In 1317, the Earl of Lancaster began to form his own army gathered from tenants of the Manor of Wakefield to fight King Edward and his favoured nobles. In 1322, the army attacked Royalist forces at Boroughbridge and was defeated and consequently executed. All men loyal to Lancaster were stripped of their lands and possessions and those not present were declared to be outlaws. Thus, were Robert Hood and a gathering of poverty-stricken fellow men reduced to seeking subsistence and survival in nearby Barnsdale Forest. Could this have been the basis of the Robin Hood tales we know today?

Sir Robert Foliot and descendents

Born 1110 - died 1165

In a fascinating book, local author Tony Molyneux-Smith put forward a new theory about the origins of the Robin Hood legend. This new approach placed the outlaw firmly back in Nottinghamshire but broke with tradition regarding his true identity.

Molyneux-Smith's conclusion is that Robin Hood was a pseudonym used by succeeding generations of a family named Foliot who held the Lordship of a place called Wellow through to the late 14th Century.

The author believes that Wellow's proximity to Sherwood Forest, together with a range of historical and geographical clues provides ample evidence for his theory. Here, it is postulated that the Foliot family used the name of Robin Hood to hide their true identities as protection against the lawless society in which they lived. These clues, together with the family's strong belief in chivalry and fair play convinced the author that Wellow and the Foliot family held the key to uncovering the truth behind the Robin Hood legend.

Robert Hod - Hobbehod

Birth and death unknown

In 1936, L.V.D. Owen put forward another candidate for the identity of Robin Hood. This theory is based on records of the York assizes which, in 1226, included 32 shillings and 6 pence for the chattels of Robert Hod fugitive. The account occurred again the following year in which the name now appeared as "Hobbehod". Through notes in the margin it can be deduced that this Robert Hod was a tenant of the archbishopric. Whilst there is no other evidence for this Robin Hood candidate, he was clearly an outlaw who had fled the juristriction of the court and remains the earliest reference discovered to date who might just be the man who sparked the legend we know and love today.

While most contemporary scholars have failed to turn up solid clues, medieval chroniclers took for granted that a historical Robin Hood lived and breathed during the 12th or 13th century. The details of their accounts vary widely, however, placing him in conflicting regions and eras. Not until John Major's "History of Greater Britain" (1521), for example, is he depicted as a follower of King Richard, one of his defining characteristics in modern times.

....

We may never know for sure whether Robin Hood ever existed outside the verses of ballads and pages of books. And even if we did, fans; young and old would still surely flock to England's Nottinghamshire region for a tour of the legend's alleged former hangouts, from centuries-old pubs to the Major Oak in Sherwood Forest.

What we do know is that the notion of a brave rebel who lives on the outskirts of society, fighting injustice and oppression with his band of companions, has universal appeal — whether he's played by Erroll Flynn, Russell Crowe or even, as on a 1979 episode of "The Muppet Show," Kermit the Frog.

The Green Children of Woolpit

The story of the Green Children of Woolpit reads rather like a typical English fairytale, but are there any elements of truth mixed in with the mythology and folk beliefs of fairies and the afterlife?

During the troubled reign of king Stephen of England (1135-1154), there was a strange occurrence in the village of Woolpit, near Bury St. Edmunds in Suffolk.

At harvest time, while the reapers were working in the fields, two young children emerged from deep ditches excavated to trap wolves, known as wolf pits (Hence the name of the village). The children, a boy and a girl, had skin tinged with a green hue, and wore clothes of a strange color, made from unfamiliar materials. They wandered around bewildered for a few minutes, before the reapers took them to the village.

Because no-one could understand the language the children spoke, they were taken to the house of local landowner Sir Richard de Calne, at Wikes. Here they broke into tears and refused to eat the bread and other food that was brought to them.

For days the children ate nothing until the villagers brought them recently harvested beans, with their stalks still attached. It was said that the children survived on this food for many months until they acquired a taste for bread.

As time passed the boy, who appeared to be the younger of the two, became depressed, sickened and died, but the girl adjusted to her new life, and was baptized. Her skin gradually lost its original green colour and she became a healthy young woman. She learned the English language and afterwards married a man at King's Lynn, in the neighbouring county of Norfolk, apparently becoming 'rather loose and wanton in her conduct'.

Some sources claim that she took the name 'Agnes Barre' and the man she married was a senior ambassador of Henry II.

It is also said that the current Earl Ferrers is descended from the strange girl through intermarriage.

What evidence this is based on is unclear, as the only traceable senior ambassador with this name at the time is Richard Barre, chancellor to Henry II, archdeacon of Ely and a royal justice in the late 12th century. After 1202, Richard retired to become an Austin canon at Leicester, so it is seems unlikely that he was the husband of 'Agnes'.

The Girl's Story

When she was later questioned about her past the girl was only able to relate vague details about where the children had come from and how they arrived at Woolpit. She stated that her and the boy were brother and sister, and had come from 'the land of Saint Martin' where it was perpetual twilight, and all the inhabitants were green in colour like they had been. She was not sure exactly where her homeland was located, but another 'luminous' land could be seen across a 'considerable river' separating it from theirs.

She remembered that one day they were looking after their father's herds in the fields and had followed them into a cavern, where they heard the loud sound of bells. Entranced, they wandered through the darkness for a long time until they arrived at the mouth of the cave, where they were immediately blinded by the glaring sunlight. They lay down in a daze for a long time, before the noise of the reapers terrified them and they rose and tried to escape, but were unable to locate the entrance of the cavern before being caught.

Green colour?

A number of ideas have been put forward to explain the strange colour of the children.

The people of Woolpit believed that the children's guardian, a Norfolk Earl, tried to poison the children with arsenic. He then left them to die in Thetford Forest on the Norfolk-Suffolk border. He would then be able to take control of their lands and money. Arsenic poisoning can make the skin a green colour. However, the children were later found, still alive but very confused and ill.

Another explanation, suggested by Paul Harris in 1998, is that they could have been children whose parents had been killed in a period of local fighting. In Eastern England there had been a lot of Flemish people coming in (immigration) during the 12th Century, but after Henry II became king, these immigrants were persecuted. In 1173, many were killed near Bury St Edmunds. He suggests the children may have been from the nearby village of Fornham St. Martin, which was separated from Woolpit by the River Lark.

Were they aliens from Mars, maybe from the fourth dimension next to ours, or were they from an anti-dimension and could they be connected to the tales of the under-race?

A scientist says that if you live underground continuously then that will bring a bluish-green color to your skin.1

Was it mere 'Green Sickness'?

The green hue of the children's skin could be the striking symptom of green sickness, the term once given to dietary deficiency anemia. In the tale, the girl is said to have lost her green tinge, which is to be expected once a healthy diet is resumed.

The Sources for the Green Children

Is there any truth behind this extraordinary story, or should it be listed among the many marvels listed by chroniclers of medieval England?

The two original sources are both from the 12th century.

William of Newburgh (1136-1198), an English historian, and monk, from Yorkshire. His main work Historia rerum Anglicarum (History of English Affairs), is a history of England from 1066 to 1198, in which he includes the story of the Green Children.

The other source is Ralph of Coggeshall (died c 1228), who was sixth abbot of Coggeshall Abbey in Essex from 1207-1218. His account of the Green Children is included in the Chronicon Anglicanum (English Chronicle) to which he contributed between 1187 and 1224. As can be seen from the dates, both authors recorded the incident many years after it was supposed to have taken place.

The fact that there is no mention of the Green Children in the Anglo-Saxon Chronicles, which deals with English history up until the death of King Stephen in 1154, and includes many of the 'wonders' popular at the time, could indicate a date for the incident early in the reign of Henry II, rather than in the reign of King Stephen.

Ralph of Coggeshall, living in Essex, the neighbouring county to Suffolk, certainly would have had direct access to the people involved in the case. In fact, he states in his Chronicle that he had frequently heard the story from Richard de Calne himself, for whom 'Agnes' worked as a servant.

In contrast, William of Newburgh, living in a remote Yorkshire monastery, would not have had such first-hand knowledge of events, though he did use contemporary historical sources, as is indicated when he says 'I was so overwhelmed by the weight of so many and such competent witnesses.

A true incident or a mere folk tale?

Gil Pérez- Teleportation from Philippines to Mexico

Mena-2Gil Pérez was a Spanish soldier of the Filipino Guardia Civil who allegedly suddenly appeared in the Plaza Mayor of Mexico City (more than 9,000 nautical miles from Manila, across the Pacific) on October 24, 1593.

He was wearing the uniform of the guards of Palacio Del Gobernador in the Philippines, and claimed he had no idea how he had arrived in Mexico. Some historians doubt the accuracy of the story, which does not appear in writing until a century after the supposed event.

Perez claimed that moments before finding himself in Mexico he had been on sentry duty in Manila at the governor's palace. He admitted that while he was aware that he was no longer in the Philippines, he had no idea where he was or how he had gotten there. He said that moments before he arrived there, His Excellency the Governor of the Philippines, Gomez Perez Dasmariñas had been killed by Chinese pirates. He explained that after long hours of duty in Manila, he felt faint, leaned against a wall and closed his eyes; he said he opened her eyes a second later to find himself somewhere different.

When it was explained to him that he was now in Mexico City, Perez refused to believe it saying that he had received his orders on the morning of October 23 in Manila and that it was therefore impossible for him to be in Mexico City on the evening of the 24th. The authorities placed Perez in jail as a deserter and for the possibility that he may have been in the service of Satan. The Most Holy Tribunal of the Inquisition questioned the soldier, but all he could say in his defense was that he had travelled from Manila to Mexico "in less time than it takes a cock to crow".

Interestingly, two months later, news from the Philippines arrived by Manila Galleon, confirming the fact of the literal axing on October 23 of Dasmariñas in a mutiny of Chinese rowers, as well as other points of the mysterious soldier's fantastic story.

Witnesses confirmed that Gil Perez had indeed been on duty in Manila just before arriving in Mexico. Furthermore, one of the passengers on the ship recognized Perez and swore that he had seen him in the Philippines on October 23.

Gil Perez eventually returned to the Philippines and took up his former position as a palace guard, living thenceforth an apparently uneventful life.

Regardless of the scientific investigations of teleportation, the story of Gil Perez is a rather scary one – particularly as he had no control over his teleportation from one place to another. Whether the story is true or not, it is a fascinating tale that has survived for hundreds of years unchanged.

The Man in the Iron Mask

The mystery of the Man in The Iron Mask has been a focal point for both doe eyed romantics and serious historians since the 17th century, generating countless theories about the identity of the masked prisoner. The interest continues even to this day, as evidenced by Di Caprio's movie. But the world is still no closer to discovering who this tragic figure was, and as the years pass, the chances of discovering of his (or her) true identity continues to fade.

Little is known about the prisoner.

What little that exists in French official documents paints a deliberately sketchy picture: he was arrested in 1669, and was imprisoned first in Pignerol, a fortress high in the French Alps. He was transferred in 1681 to Exiles, which lay close to Pignerol, and in 1687 he was moved yet again to the southern French coastal island of Saint Marguerite. His stay on the island lasted eleven years until he was sent to the Bastille in Paris. Finally, the prisoner died in 1703, an undoubtedly welcome release.

Throughout his entire imprisonment, there were reportedly only two instances of witnesses outside of prison officials actually seeing the prisoner. During his move from Exiles to Saint Marguerite, the prisoner was seen wearing a steel mask. With the move to the Bastille, this cumbersome disguise was replaced with a more humane mask of black velvet. It has also been discovered through official correspondence between a government minister and Saint Mars, the prisoner's jailer, that the prisoner was not to communicate with anyone, be it by writing or speaking. If he did, he was to be executed on the spot.

What terrible secret could this man have possessed that demanded such secrecy?

Historians have wondered why he was even kept alive: if the knowledge he held was of such danger to the King and government, wouldn't it have been politically safer simply to kill him? And why such a concern over people seeing his face?

Did he resemble someone well known to the French populace, which would have to make him famous indeed, considering the primitive state of print media during the 17th century? Once again, simply killing him — an option not in disuse in the French court of the time — would have made more sense.

THE STRANGE PART

Saint Mars, the man appointed to jail the mysterious prisoner, held that position from the first day of his incarceration until the prisoner breathed his last in 1703. Given the usual turnstile approach to political appointments, this constancy is intriguing.

LEGENDS

**The mask was made of iron. Voltaire, writing in 1751, said it was riveted on, and described in detail a "movable, hinged lower jaw held in place by springs that made it possible to eat wearing it." The only reliable contemporary reference we have to the mask clearly calls it black velvet, not iron, but the "iron mask" caught the public's imagination.

**That there were two soldiers always at his side ready to shoot him if he ever unmasked.

**That he was treated with extreme courtesy by his jailors. The governor of the prison personally took care of his linens and meals. The governor and jailors removed their hats in his presence, remained standing until he invited them to sit, served his meals on silver plate, and so forth--in short, etiquette accorded royalty. This legend was widespread, and makes a great story, but prison records show exactly what supplies were furnished--and they were pretty humble.

Rooms in the Bastille before 1745 were unfurnished, as the majority of political prisoners preferred to provide their own furnishings. Du Junca's notebooks record that the masked prisoner had no furniture of his own, instead using the standard furniture provided by the governor. This implies that the Man in the Mask was not wealthy, and certainly wasn't treated "like royalty."

**The prisoner wrote a message with the point of a knife on a silver plate, and tossed the plate out the window into the river. It was found by a fisherman who brought it back to the prison, and was immediately questioned by the governor whether he had read what was on the plate. He said that he did not know how to read. He was imprisoned and interrogated and investigated, and it was proved that he had no schooling and could not read or write his own name.

The governor then freed him, saying, "It is your great luck that you can't read!"

This story was recounted by Voltaire in the 1750s.

A similar story is told about a shirt of fine quality, covered with writing, found by a barber and returned to Saint-Mars; two day later, the barber was dead.

THE USUAL SUSPECTS

Louis XIV

Many fingers point towards the King of France. The masked prisoner could have been the twin brother of Louis, rumored to have been conceived first but unfortunately born last. His true identity hidden from the twin to clear up any messy succession procedures, Louis would have imprisoned him once he discovered who he was.

Other theories feel that he could have been an elder brother, the result of an extramarital affair of Louis' mother.

Another theory states the prisoner was an attending doctor at Louis XIII's autopsy, who unfortunately discovered the late king incapable of siring children, thus endangering Louis XIV's own right to the throne.

Following the same thread, the prisoner could have been the true father of Louis, recruited due to the previous king's inability in the bedroom, hidden to stave off political turmoil.

Count Antonio Matthioli

He may have been the prisoner, wearing the mask for the most pointless of reasons: because it was the fashionable thing to do in Italy at the time.

Matthioli was an unscrupulous politician from Mantua, in Italy, who was involved in negotiations between the Duke of Mantua and the Republic of Venice, using France as an intermediary. (At the time, remember, Italy was not unified but comprised a large number of small but powerful states.) Matthioli double-crossed everyone in sight, and "caused disturbances in at least five countries, which came near leading to general war," according to van Keler. This put the King of France in a very awkward position.

Matthioli was kidnapped by the French in May 1679 in Italy and hustled off to the mountain fortress of Pignerol. The arrest warrant contained a postscript: "No person shall know what has become of this man" by special order of the King. The French secretary of state, Louvois, instructed the governor to give him only absolute necessities, and nothing of comfort, saying this was at the special request of the King. Matthioli almost became deranged from this treatment.

He did not accompany Saint-Mars when he was transferred to the prison at Exiles in 1681, but was transferred to the prison at Sainte Marguerite in March 1694, so meets our criteria. After 1694, Mattioli disappears from official correspondence.

Louis Oldendorff

A Lorraine nobleman, Oldendorff was the leader of the Secret Order of the Temple. The rules of this society would not allow them to replace him while he still lived. After he died, another man was made to wear the mask, thus maintaining the illusion of Oldendorff's imprisonment, and keeping the Order from selecting a new leader.

Eustace Dauger

The more likely candidate is a prisoner named Eustace Dauger (or some similar spelling), who was a valet. The name Dauger is likely false, and there is considerable speculation about who Dauger might have been. The King's arrest warrant restricts Dauger from having any contact with anyone.

Saint-Mars himself must feed Dauger, and the secretary of state writes to Saint-Mars, "You must never, under any pretenses, listen to what he may wish to tell you. You must threaten him with death if he speaks one word except about his actual needs. He is only a valet, and does not need much furniture."

Dauger was transferred from Pignerol with Saint-Mars to Exiles in 1681 and to Sainte Marguerite in 1687, so meets the criteria.

Also suspected to be the prisoner: Richard Cromwell; the Duke of Monmouth; Vivien de Bulonde

THE UNUSUAL SUSPECTS

Hidden Daughter of Louis XIII and Anne

Terrified of not having a son, the elder Louis may have hidden his newborn daughter and replaced her with an infant boy changeling. When she discovered her identity, Louis XIV (the changeling) had her imprisoned.

Moliere

As beloved as the playwright was both by the French public and Louis XIV, Moliere made many enemies because of his lack of religious beliefs and disdain for the French establishment. He especially angered the Company of the Holy Sacrament, a strong and influential Catholic group.

The theory follows that Moliere's death was staged in 1673, with the playwright becoming The Man in the Iron Mask as punishment.

Nicholas Fouquet

Fouquet was allegedly imprisoned for discovering hidden knowledge that Christ didn't die on the cross, but survived, leading to a secret bloodline of direct ancestors.

Napoleon Bonaparte

Napoleon Bonaparte, who claimed to be a direct descendent of the king, embraced a popular theory that claimed the king's older brother had been imprisoned in order to assure that Louis XIV would be the sole king. While imprisoned, however, the man was allowed to marry and subsequently fathered a son who was sent away to be raised in Corsica. The name of the family who took in this hapless child was supposedly Bonaparte. While the theory suited Napoleon's needs, no evidence exists that suggests it could be true.

MOST CONVINCING EVIDENCE

The fact that the prisoner wasn't simply killed indicates that there must have been a royal connection. Anyone else would have been left to an unmarked grave or garotte.

MOST MYSTERIOUS FACT

Despite the backstabbing of French politics, despite the gains that could be made by revealing who this prisoner was, despite methodical examination of records, there is no indication of who the prisoner was. It was a universally kept secret, by all parties involved.

SCEPTICALLY SPEAKING

The identity of the Man in the Iron Mask is so well hidden one can surmise it's simply because he didn't exist at all. The vision of such a figure would go far in quelling any dissidents to the King's rule. The prospect of lifelong imprisonment will do that.

Who was he? Was he a myth? No one knows till today.

Scary Shadow People

"WHAT WAS THAT?" You were sitting comfortably on your sofa reading in the dim light when movement across the room caught your attention. It seemed dark and shadowy, but there was nothing there. You returned to your reading - and a moment later there it was again. You looked up quickly this time and saw the fleeting but distinctly human shape of the shadow pass quickly over the far wall... and disappear.

What was that?

Some natural shadow?

Your heightened imagination?

A ghost?

Or was it something that seems to be a spreading phenomenon - apparitions that are coming to be known as "shadow people" or "shadow beings."

What Are They?

Some believe shadow people are compassionate guardians while others think they are evil beings. So far, no one has produced any conclusive evidence of what they are.

Speculation abounds, but several theories have been put forth. People have called them "shadow people" since most sightings report them as having a human like form.

Overactive imaginations may account for some reports, but you can't account for the number of similar details as mere coincidence.

Some believe shadow people are merely one form of ghost who has passed on. Others believe they are evil beings meaning to cause harm. Still others believe they are inter-dimensional beings slipping into our world on occasion.

Could they be time travelers? And then, there is the inevitable space alien theory.

Shadow people are often mistaken to be ghosts, but they are totally different. Ghosts are said to be spirits of deceased human beings that take on human manifestations and attributes.

However, they differ from the common ghost description having discernable physical characteristics including clothing. Shadow people are also described as being featureless. Their movements have been generally reported to be quick and disjointed but have been seen to move in slow motion. Accounts sometimes portray a totally black being with red eyes, a cloak, and hat.

Research reveals the movement of shadow people to be quick and jerky, sometimes with stops, starts, not like floating motions associated with ghost sighting. Unlike ghost sightings, encounters with shadow people are almost always frightening.

Witnesses claiming to have had encounters with these mysterious occurrences express feeling an ominous presence or a sense of being watched. When they turn to look it disappears into thin air, or escapes through a wall. Reports say they don't appear to reflect light and are essentially a silhouette in black.

Their personalities are sometimes said to be curious and childlike, and seem to play cat and mouse games with observers. Other times people sense their presence as being pure evil.

Origin of shadow people

The nature and origin of shadow people at present are unknown. Some believe they are inter-dimensional beings existing in a parallel dimension. Others hypothesize they are demonic entities. It has even been suggested they may be thought forms created by negative psychic energy related to a place where extreme, emotional incidents have taken place.

Some conditions reported are similar to occurrences in episodes of sleep paralysis. Witnesses to shadow people appearances report experiences occur just before falling asleep, or after waking. Reports of being held down in bed are not uncommon.

However, this could be a condition called hypnagogic paralysis. This is a condition where a state of paralysis occurs during REM sleep in order to keep a person from acting out their dreams physically.

A temporary paralysis can occur when suddenly awakened from an REM state. At this point a person can be fully aware, but unable to move. While in this state a person can subconsciously have vivid hallucinations including sensory perceptions such as taste, smell, auditory, physical and visual phenomena.

Observers frequently report glimpsing shadow people through their peripheral vision. Peripheral vision is linked to the area of the brain that distinguishes familiar patterns.

And in a condition known as pareidolia, the brain can also falsely interpret random patterns of light, shadow or texture as familiar patterns such as faces or bodies. It has also been found electro-magnetic fields can sometimes affect functions of the temporal lobe creating altered states of perception.

Some have categorized them as-

Benign Shadows: Shadow People that seem to travel briefly through a person's life.

Negative Shadows: Although these Shadow People tend to simply lurk, they are associated with a feeling of unnatural terror.

Red-Eyed Shadows: These entities are always negative, but stare at experiencer with blazing red eyes. Victims often say they feel this creature feed from their fear.

Hooded Shadows: Dressed as an ancient monk, people who encounter these Shadow People feel a deep rage bubbling behind the black cowl.

The Hat Man: This entity is the most curious. Dressed in a fedora, and sometimes appearing to wear an old-time business suit, the Hat Man appears to people in cultures across the planet.

Fortunately, shadow people don't seem to be dangerous, although they project an overwhelming sense of fear and dread. Whatever they are, there have been countless reports by people around the world.

Do they really exist, no one can say.

DB Cooper

The particulars of D.B. Cooper's clever airborne crime and daredevil getaway have been pondered, picked over and recapitulated for three decades now.

In 1971, D.B. Cooper hijacked and threatened to blow up an airliner, extorted $200,000 from its owner, Northwest Orient, then leaped from the airborne 727 with 21 pounds of $20 bills strapped to his torso.

He was never seen again—dead or alive. The crime was perfect if he lived, perfectly crazy if he didn't.

In either case, D.B. Cooper's nom de crime—no one knows his real name—may be the most recognized alias among western felons since Jack the Ripper.

Everyone from dour G-men to giddy amateur sleuths have pored over the details, hoping to wheedle a resolution out of some overlooked aspect, as though a clue concealed in the holdup's hieroglyph of facts might lead to an a-ha! a la Inspector Clouseau.

Yet the case remains unsolved more than 30 years later, and D. B. Cooper has become the Bigfoot of crime, evading one of the most extensive and expensive American manhunts of the 20thcentury. The whereabouts of the man (or his remains) is one of the great crime mysteries of our time.

D.B. Cooper's crime was different. First, no innocent bystander was injured, although law enforcers argue that he put several dozen lives at risk.

There was modest collateral damage to Northwest Orient's bottom line, and the FBI's swollen ego was bruised to the bone. Cooper pulled his buccaneering swipe in the twilight of the 47-year tenure of FBI Director J. Edgar Hoover, who died not long after the hijacking. The director no doubt went to his grave with teeth gritted over his agency's inability, in this case, to get their man.

Cooper's crime also was unusual in that it helped rally critical support for sweeping air travel security initiatives, including passenger screening. Until D. B. Cooper's skydive, it was entirely possible to walk aboard a jet carrying a bomb.

Most law-abiders react with revulsion to violent criminals, with disgust to extortionists, and with a tsk-tsk to the preponderate larcenies that fill crime blotters in police stations across America.

Yet Cooper induced more smiles than frowns.

But did D. B. Cooper get away with it? No one can say for certain. We do know that he could have survived the dangerous nighttime skydive because Cooper's caper, like a crime science experiment, was replicated with complete success by a copycat aerial clip artist just months later. That hijacker hit the ground safely, although the mimic ultimately paid dearly. The copycat case also spawned a controversial theory about the fate of Dan Cooper.

Coincidentally, Cooper himself probably copied a similar hijacking that occurred two weeks before his endeavor.

Dr Barry's Deathbed s*x secret

On the morning of July 25, 1865, just after dawn, a loud scream rang out around the great physician's deathbed.

Dr James Barry had not been an easy patient. A man as cantankerous as he was brilliant, few dared argue with the Inspector General of Military Hospitals, so for the past month his curtains had been kept drawn, ensuring his bedroom on London's Cavendish Square was in a state of perpetual half-light.

But now he was dead, Sophia Bishop, the charwoman sent to prepare his corpse, had no intention of complying with his final wish, which was that on no account should he be changed out of the clothes in which he had died.

"The devil!" cried Sophia as she pulled up his nightshirt to wash his body and, quite literally, uncovered a secret the doctor had managed to hide for most of his life.

"It's a woman - and [noting what she took for stretch marks on his stomach] a woman that has had a child."

This truth was so scandalous to Victorian Britain that for years it was hushed up.

Dr James Barry was one of the most highly respected surgeons of his day. He had risen from hospital assistant to become the top-ranking doctor in the British Army and was known as a zealous reformer who had served in garrisons from South Africa to Jamaica.

He performed one of the first successful Caesarean sections

in medical history, was summoned by Napoleon to attend to the son of his private secretary and, thanks to his careful subterfuge, was the first woman to practice medicine in Britain.

Despite "a most peculiar squeaky voice and mincing manner", as one ambassador's daughter noted, Dr Barry's fierce temper ensured he was a force to be reckoned with.

He even crossed swords with another leading medical figure of his day, Florence Nightingale, who later described him as "a brute" and "the most hardened creature I ever met throughout the Army".

Just how exactly did he - or she, as perhaps we ought to call her - pull off this lifelong charade?

New research among a cache of letters, accounts and legal documents has helped to make sense of the extraordinary life of Dr James Barry.

Over the decades, a range of conditions, including that she was a hermaphrodite, have been suggested to explain away Dr Barry's ability to have begun life as a female, yet successfully persuade everyone that she was a man.

But the truth is she was simply a woman, born in Ireland as Margaret Ann Bulkley sometime in the 1790s, the daughter of Mary-Ann and Jeremiah, a greengrocer from Cork.

In 1803, Jeremiah Bulkley was sent to prison for debt and his wife turned to her brother, the famous artist James Barry, to help ease the family's financial troubles.

Barry was part of a liberal, forward-thinking set who were keen believers in women's rights and education, and when he died in 1806, leaving some money to the Bulkleys, his influential friends gladly took Margaret and her mother under their wing.

The Bulkleys moved first to London, where Margaret began to take lessons from the physician Edward Fryer.

Margaret proved an able pupil and before long an even more elaborate, if not preposterously ambitious, plan had been hatched for her future.

At that time, women were not permitted to enter university, so it was decided that she would masquerade as a man and train as a doctor.

In 1809, Margaret - assuming her uncle's name, James Barry - sailed from London to Edinburgh where she planned to enrol at the university as a medical student, and she and her mother intended to establish themselves as aunt and nephew.

"It was very useful for Mrs Bulkley to have a gentleman to take care of her on board ship," Barry wrote to one of her sponsors.

The establishment of a new life was total. Mother and daughter isolated themselves from anyone who might not be trusted to keep this darkest of secrets.

Margaret wore an overcoat to disguise her womanly curves, and fibbed about her age as a means of explaining her smooth chin and high voice.

She graduated three years later, moved back to London for a six-month stint as an apprentice surgeon at St Thomas's Hospital and, in 1813, joined the Army.

She was a misfit from the start: less than 5ft tall, she wore stacked heels and had to have 3in soles fastened to her boots to give her elevation.

But the flamboyant styles of the day - men dressed effeminately as a fashion, not a sexual statement - worked in her favour.

In 1816 Barry was posted to the colony on the Cape of Good Hope in South Africa.

There, she acquired a black manservant who would stay with her for the next 50 years, and whose trusted task it was to lay out six small towels each morning that she would use like bandages to disguise her curves and broaden her slender shoulders.

She rapidly became known for her foibles, which included sleeping every night with a black poodle called Psyche, riding about in dress uniform wearing a cavalry sword and taking a goat everywhere so she could drink its milk.

She also acquired a reputation as a ladies' man, perhaps believing this would give her better cover.

As fearless in her professional as she was in her personal life, Barry instigated a sweeping series of reforms, campaigning against poor sanitation and overcrowding in the Cape's prisons, and for lepers as well as the soldiers it was her duty to look after.

In Lord Charles Somerset, the governor of the colony, who became a close friend and, possibly, also a confidant and lover, she had a powerful ally whose protection must have helped to repel any uneasy rumours.

Barry's sharp tongue and fierce redhead's temper did the rest.

For a period of about one year - around 1819 - Barry disappeared.

Afterwards she claimed to have been sent to Mauritius, but some historians believe she may have fallen pregnant and given birth to a stillborn child.

But she returned, and in 1826 cemented her reputation as a master surgeon when, despite knowing that no woman in Britain had ever survived the procedure, she conducted an emergency Caesarean on one Mrs Munnik - on her kitchen table - and saved her life as well as the baby's.

Barry remained in South Africa until 1828, when she embarked on a series of postings to Mauritius, Jamaica and St Helena, among other places.

By 1845 Barry was serving as principal medical officer in the West Indies, where she contracted a terrible bout of yellow fever.

Convinced she was not going to survive, she laid down strict instructions that her unexamined body should be left in a nightshirt and wrapped in a winding sheet.

In fact, she did recover, and when the Crimean War broke out, she demanded to be sent to the front line.

Her request was refused and, instead, she was stationed in Corfu to tend to the wounded when they had been shipped out there.

With typical determination, Barry used her leave to go to the Crimea anyway, and this is how she came to meet Florence Nightingale.

On paper, these two great pioneering reformers with

identical concerns about sanitation should have got on famously; instead, thanks to Barry's outspoken manner, they had a furious row.

In 1857 Barry was sent to Canada and promoted to the post of inspector-general of hospitals.

However, a career in the tropics, and the onset of old age, had not equipped her for the freezing winters. She suffered with flu and bronchitis and was forced to retire.

Along with her loyal servant from South Africa, she came back to London and it was there that she succumbed to a diarrhoea epidemic that eventually killed her.

Right until the end Barry had done everything to prevent her secret from being discovered, even requesting that no post-mortem be carried out on her corpse.

In the end, though, our knowledge of it only makes a life already noteworthy even more remarkable.

The strange case of Rudolph Fentz

The story:

In 1950, a man with mutton chop sideburns and Victorian-era duds popped up in Times Square. Witnesses said he looked startled, and then a minute later, he was hit by a car and killed.

The officials at the morgue searched his body and found the following items in his pockets:

A copper token for a beer worth 5 cents, bearing the name of a saloon, which was unknown, even to older residents of the area

A bill for the care of a horse and the washing of a carriage, drawn by a livery stable on Lexington Avenue that was not listed in any address book

About 70 dollars in old banknotes

Business cards with the name Rudolph Fentz and an address on Fifth Avenue

A letter sent to this address, in June 1876 from Philadelphia

None of these objects showed any signs of aging.

Captain Hubert V. Rihm of the Missing Persons Department of NYPD tried using this information to identify the man. He found that the address on Fifth Avenue was part of a business; its current owner did not know Rudolph Fentz. Fentz's name was not listed in the address book, his fingerprints were not recorded anywhere, and no one had reported him missing.

Rihm continued the investigation and finally found a Rudolph Fentz Jr. in a telephone book of 1939. Rihm spoke to the residents of the apartment building at the listed address who remembered Fentz and described him as a man about 60 years who had worked nearby. After his retirement, he moved to an unknown location in 1940.

Contacting the bank, Rihm was told that Fentz died five years before, but his widow was still alive but lived in Florida. Rihm contacted her and learned that her husband's father had disappeared in 1876 aged 29. He had left the house for an evening walk and never returned

The facts:

The story was published a number of times in the 70's and 80's as fact, until 2000, after the Spanish magazine 'Más Allá' published a representation of the events as a factual report, folklore researcher Chris Aubeck investigated the description to check the veracity. His research, led to the conclusion that the people and events of the story invented all were fictional, although he could not find the original source.

Pastor George Murphy claimed in 2002 that the original source was from either a 1952 Robert Heinlein science fiction anthology, entitled 'Tomorrow, The Stars' or the Collier's magazine from 15 September 1951. The true author was the renowned science fiction writer Jack Finney (1911–1995), and the Fentz episode was part of the short story I'm Scared, which was published in Collier's first. This meant that the fictional character and the source of the story were finally identified – so everyone thought. No copies of the story have ever been found, and Finney died before he could be questioned.

The Twist

In 2007 a researcher working for the then Berlin News Archive, found a newspaper story in the archives from April 1951 reporting the story almost as it reported today. This newspaper archive was printed some 5 months before the short story sourced as the origin. Whats even odder, a number of researchers have claimed to have found evidence of the real Rudolph Fentz, and proof of his disappearance aged 29 in 1876.

HIDDEN TREASURES

- *Holy Grail*

- *The Knights Templar*

Holy Grail

Almost all of our understanding of the Holy Grail is derived from romantic Arthurian tales of the twelfth and thirteenth centuries.

However, there are some generally accepted details.

The Grail is believed to be the chalice of the Eucharist or dish of the Pascal lamb used by Christ at the Last Supper. This vessel was taken by Joseph of Arimathea, who used it to collect blood from the crucified body of Christ.

An alternative theory is that it was a chalice given to Joseph by Christ in a vision. This vessel's holy powers sustained Joseph for 42 years during his incarceration by the Jews.

In either case, Joseph brought the holy chalice to Britain, thus beginning the true legend.

Some people believe the Holy Grail was secretly passed down through generations of Joseph's descendants. Others believe it is buried in the Chalice Well at Britain's oldest holy city, Glastonbury, which indicates a connection to Arthurian legend.

Romantic tales say that Arthur and his Knights of the Round Table set off on a holy quest to find the Grail.

More reliable legend says the Cathars had possession of the Grail and hid it in the Pyrenees before they were over-run.

It has been suggested that they may have kept it at their stronghold of Montségur, which was actually searched by

Nazi forces looking for the Grail during the Second World War.

Others believe the Cathars hid it at Rennes-le-Château, or gave the chalice to the Knights Templar for safe-keeping.

Some researchers believe a field in Shropshire hides the Grail under its surface, and another tradition states that a wooden cup in a Welsh country house is the true artifact.

The organized church does not credit any legend of its existence, although that should not be seen as any indication that it is purely a myth.

Whether any evidence of the fabled chalice's existence is ever found or not, the story of the Holy Grail will continue to puzzle Man for many years to come.

The Knights Templar

A group of French knights founded an order in Jerusalem in 1118 under the title 'The Poor Fellow-Soldiers of Christ'.

The warriors all took monastic views and pledged their lives to protecting Christian travelers and the Holy Land. They were housed at the palace of King Baldwin II, the French King of Jerusalem, on the site of Solomon's Temple which is how they gained their title 'Knights Templar'.

In 1128 they were officially sanctioned by Pope Honorius II, and they were provided with a 'Rule' from Saint Bernard of Clairvaux. The knights gained a fearsome reputation for being ferocious in battle, courageous and honourable. They fought in the Crusades alongside Richard the Lionheart and quickly accumulated vast amounts of treasure, wealth and land from grateful European monarchs.

Within 200 years the Templars had left the Holy Land and taken residence in Paris, but such was their influence that they were only required to answer to the Pope. Their riches were so immense that they began the earliest form of organised banking, and became known as moneylenders to European monarchies.

But this, combined with a history of holding meetings in secret, led to their downfall.

King Philip the Fair of France was known to be hugely indebted with staggering sums owed to the order. On 13th October 1307, he declared that the Templars engaged in heretical activities at their meetings, arrested all members of the order in France, and seized their assets.

The Templars accepted his decisions quietly, but many were then tortured into giving false confessions of unholy practices. However, only the Pope could condemn the order, and a newly installed Pope Clement V was happy to bow to Philip's coercions. The order was disbanded, and it was suggested that all European monarchies take steps to suppress the movement.

On 19th March 1314, the last Grand Master of the Knights Templar, Jacques de Molay, was burned at the stake on an island in the middle of the River Seine in Paris. As the flames rose, it is claimed de Molay cursed King Philip and Pope threatening that they would both follow him within a year. They both did - Clement died a month later and Philip seven months after that.

However, the Knights Templar themselves are said to have continued in secret, and before his death, de Molay had passed on his powers to a successor.

Some of the Templars are believed to have taken refuge in Scotland during the intervening years, but the movement did not reveal itself again until 1705. Since then the order has had associations with Freemasonry and other secret societies, but the movement has flourished and they have had many high profile and influential members.

In more recent years, following the Second World War, the cohesion of the entire international order has become somewhat fractured. The meetings are still held in secret. Apart from fiercely guarded rituals and traditions, it would seem that there are few mysteries surrounding the order. But one question remains - why did the Parisian Templars not fight when arrested by Philip's men? In the days leading to their capture, a heavily-laden cart was supposedly removed from their buildings.

Philip never found all the riches in their offices that he wished to acquire, and it seems the knights submitted to his thuggery meekly, in order to let their great treasure escape.

So, what was this treasure?

The obvious theory is that it was gold and jewels taken from holy temples of Jerusalem and the biblical world during the Crusades. However, many have speculated that the reaction of the Templars suggested that it was something beyond material value, and may have been something of enormous spiritual importance, such as the Ark of the Covenant or the Holy Grail.

Others have considered that it may be secret Christian knowledge, such as the 'bloodline of Jesus Christ'. The treasure, whatever nature it takes, has never been found, and where it is hidden remains a mystery.

Many Templar experts have considered it may have been the root of Bérenger Saunière's mysterious wealth, and believe it was buried at the church of Rennes-le-Château.

However, one of the most widely-held theories is that the surviving Templars hid it at Rosslyn Chapel in Scotland.

If the order did manage to continue throughout its banished years, there is good reason to believe the secrets of the treasure are known to only a select few. To the rest of us, the Knights Templar are only modern-day descendants of a historical mystery.

COMMUNICATIONS

- *Nazca Lines*

- *The Piri Reis Map*

- *Ancient Astronauts*

Nazca Lines

The Nazca lines are geoglyphs and geometric line clearings in the Peruvian desert. They were made by the Nazca people, who flourished between 200 BCE and 600 CE along rivers and streams that flow from the Andes. The desert itself runs for over 1,400 miles along the Pacific Ocean. The area of the Nazca art is called the Pampa Colorado (Red Plain). It is 15 miles wide and runs some 37 miles parallel to the Andes and the sea.

Dark red surface stones and soil have been cleared away, exposing the lighter-colored subsoil, creating the "lines". There is no sand in this desert.

From the air, the "lines" include not only lines and geometric shapes, but also depictions of animals and plants in stylized forms. Some of the forms, including images of humans, grace the steep hillsides at the edge of the desert.

Locals had always known of the strange marks found on the dusty floor, although it was only now, the discovery sparked an interest and a study that continues to this day: people wanted to know why they were there, and what they meant.

The pictures themselves were created using the gravel, soil and distinctly colored under crust.

Because the area experiences less than an inch of rainfall each year, and the effect of the wind on the surface is minimal, the shapes have been preserved over centuries. There are over 100 outlines of animals and plants, including a monkey, spider, hummingbird and even, it is thought, a spaceman.

Countless straight lines form squares, triangles, trapezoids and all manner of strange angles. They seem to run in random directions and to random lengths – one even stretches for nine miles along the desert floor.

Over 3,000 years ago the area was inhabited by a race called the Nazca, who had developed proficient techniques in pottery, weaving and architecture. They created highly effective irrigation systems and successfully grew crops in a harsh environment.

It is widely believed that these people were responsible for drawing the lines, although the actual date of the lines' creation is impossible to determine.

A nearby city called Cahauchi, just south of the lines, was recently discovered as being the probable home of the Nazcan line drawers.

Experts were able to deduce that the majority of Nazcan people fled the city after a series of natural disasters, with the few native people who remained being exiled or killed by Spanish conquistadors.

Excavations in the surrounding mountains are uncovering extraordinary clues about the people who made them and why. A long since vanished people, called the Nasca, flourished here between 200BC and 700AD. But the harsh environment led them to extreme measures in order to survive.

Archaeologist Christina Conlee recently made an extraordinary find: the skeleton of a young male, ceremonially buried but showing gruesome evidence of decapitation. In place of the missing human head, a ceramic "head jar" decorated with a striking image of a decapitated head with a tree sprouting from its skull.

Conlee wonders who this person was? Why was he beheaded and yet buried with honor. Was he a captive taken in battle, or could he have been a willing sacrifice? And did his decapitation have anything to do with the lines? The discovery of large caches of human heads adds grisly weight to Conlee's theories and helps unravel on of man's great mysteries.

But why would a race want to draw pictures that could only be appreciated from the sky?

Perhaps the most celebrated theory was the one advanced by Dr Maria Reiche. She tried to prove that the lines correlated to important stars rising in the heavens, and the symbols of animals were actually native representations of star constellations. But her views were not universally supported due to the very fact that the lines cannot be dated.

As the Earth's relationship with the universe turns, any line in any direction will correspond to some astronomical feature at some date. After a lifetime of study and fascination, Reiche died and was buried in the Nazca valley in 1998.

During the 1960s, writers such as Louis Pauwels, Jacques Bergier, and Erich von Daniken famously promoted ideas that the lines were runways or landing strip for alien visitors.

Other theories suggest they are an astronomical calendar; that they were used for religious ceremonies; or that they indicated underground sources of water.

One expert believes that, before the invention of weaving tools, the lines had men standing along them holding thread, in a version of a giant human loom. But exactly why the images were designed to be viewed from the air has never really been addressed.

One quite astonishing theory is that the Nazca people were the original human aviators, and had developed the first rudimentary hot air balloon.

Our understanding of the Nazcan culture has developed with archaeological discoveries, but today the fate of the lines is in serious jeopardy.

In recent years, political and advertising agencies have graphitized slogans on the patterns, whilst a recent surge in gold and copper mining in the area is defacing the designs with industrial activities and heavy traffic movements.

The expanding local population needs a higher level of basic amenities, which has meant utility providers are now running cables and pipes over the site. Combined with the effects of natural weathering, this means that the most enigmatic and mysterious visual display of an ancient race is under threat of being lost from Man's history forever.

The Piri Reis Map:

The story begins in 1929, when the new republican government of Turkey was converting the old Topkapi Palace in Istanbul into a museum. During the work, a map was discovered that was more than 400 years old but had been hitherto unknown. (That in itself is not necessarily surprising: maps of that era were state secrets.) The map was the western third of a portolan chart of the world, drawn on gazelle skin. It covered the Americas, the Atlantic Ocean, the Iberian Peninsula and the western part of Africa. The rest of the chart, covering the Mediterranean Sea, Indian Ocean and Far East, is presumably lost forever.

The map was the handiwork of an Ottoman admiral named Piri Reis ("Reis" was his rank — admiral), who in 1513 compiled the map from many different sources — some ancient, some more recent, including Portuguese charts of Asia and charts made by Columbus that were obtained by his uncle in 1501 when he captured seven Spanish ships.

Ironically, it is the map's correctness and reliability that has since become the issue.

Piri Reis's map, fascinating on its own, now leaves the realm of 15th-century navigators and enters the lands of ancient astronauts, ice-age civilizations, and shifting poles.

Enter Charles Hapgood, who uses the Piri Reis map to argue, in his 1966 book, Maps of the Ancient Sea Kings, a number of extraordinary things. Hapgood saw, at the bottom left of the map, what he believed to be an accurate representation of the ice-free coast of Antarctica.

He fit that into his pre-existing theory that the Earth's poles had shifted in the relatively recent past (or, of you like, that the Earth's crust had shifted relative to the poles), leaving Antarctica ice-free, and that, 9,500 years ago, there was an advanced civilization that accurately mapped the Antarctic coastline. And that among Piri Reis's ancient sources were maps from that civilization.

Many Piri Reis Map enthusiasts believe the level of geographical detail and mathematical knowledge needed to create the map was far beyond the reach of navigators from the sixteenth or earlier centuries.

Indeed, experts at the United States Air Force in the 1960s found the map so accurate they used it to replace false information on their own charts.

Some people believe the map could only have been achieved with the help of aerial surveys, and suggest alien creatures mapped the planet thousands of years ago, leaving their results behind to be copied by Mankind.

The map's seemingly accurate depiction of the geography of Antarctica is its most fascinating aspect. Antarctica was discovered in 1818, and the actual land of the continent was only mapped in 1949 by a combined British and Scandinavian project that had to use modern equipment to see the land underneath the mile-deep icecap.

The theory put forward to compensate for this is that an ancient race using advanced, but now lost, technology was able to accurately record details of the continent before it was covered with ice.

Most experts suggest Antarctica was icefree no later than 6,000 years ago, although others believe ice has covered the continent for – at least – hundreds of thousands of years.

Similarly, many cartography experts claim the accuracy of the portolan system of map drawing is more in the eye of the beholder, and many maps of this time included imaginary continents in the south Atlantic. But there are still some unexplainably accurate details on the map.

The Falkland Islands are placed at the correct latitude, despite not being discovered until 1592, and the unknown Andes mountain range was included on the map of America. Similarly, Greenland was shown as three separate islands, a fact only discovered this century. So, the debate continues. Did Piri Reis just strike lucky with cartographic guesswork? Or did the Turkish admiral have access to charts and maps created by an advanced race, living on the planet thousands of years ago?

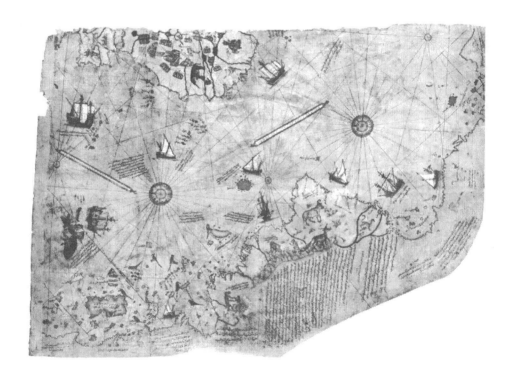

Ancient Astronauts

Daniken's book 'Chariots of the Gods' has many followers who believe it is the most convincing text supporting the idea of alien travelers instigating mankind's traditions. He claims that the first UFOs ever to visit the Earth landed in prehistoric times, and the aliens that alighted were really the beings responsible for our ancient ancestor's intelligence. Such a theory encompasses countless tales of ancient, now lost, races.

The legends of Lemuria, Atlantis and Nazca all have elements that encourage intergalactic relationships, and Daniken's daring suggestions have spurred countless similar theories linking our history with visits from ancient astronauts.

Daniken was born on 14th April 1935 in Zofingen, Switzerland. At school he was fascinated by ancient holy writings, but it was during his time managing a Swiss hotel that he wrote his first and most famous book, 'Chariots of the Gods'. The book looked at evidence to support a theory that prehistoric Man did not have the abilities to create his own civilizations. Daniken stated that ancient astronauts had arrived on the planet and introduced our ancestors' culture, traditions and intelligence. By carefully choosing data from religious, historical, scientific, biological, and mythical and even some downright fictional sources, Daniken created a compelling argument.

But many other experts have since had to question his assertions.

He claimed that the Ark of the Covenant was made as a large electric capacitor, when in fact its design is utterly impractical.

Famously, he stated that the fabled Nazca lines are runways for alien spacecraft, but did not consider the other options: for example, that they might have something to do with native Nazcan culture. He introduced impossible equations and even fictional 'facts'.

One example of Daniken's evidence was pottery said to date from Biblical times. The ancient pots had pictures of UFOs painted in their sides, but a television documentary team found the potter who created the artifacts.

When Daniken was confronted with proof of his fraud, he replied that it was allowed because some people will irrationally refuse to believe an argument unless they see tangible evidence. Since then, rival or complementary theories about similar subjects have appeared.

Another controversial notion was written by Robert Bauval and Adrian Gilbert in their 1994 book 'The Orion Mystery'.

The idea is termed 'The Orion Theory', and is solely connected with the belief that the Ancient Egyptians are descended from alien visitors.

Gilbert and Bauval realized that the three pyramids at Giza correlate exactly with the three belt stars of Orion. Subsequent study using the theory has apparently discovered other ancient structures in areas of Egypt that correspond to points of the Orion constellation. The Orion Theory suggests that the alien visitors originated from a planet in the Orion constellation. The Egyptians worshipped the god Osiris, who had 'Sha' as its cosmic representation. The Sha constellation is what we call Orion.

Gilbert and Bauval also studied the strange shafts found in

the pyramids which they said were directed towards the right area of the heavens for the dead pharaohs' souls to ascend back from whence they came.

Modern scholars have pointed out that the Earth's position and view of the heavens would have been drastically different in ancient history, and suspicious manipulation of time frames has been used to make sure some related theories are seen as plausible.

In reality, this has undermined the integrity of the whole subject.

FASCINATING MONUMENTS

- *Iron Pillar of Delhi*

Iron Pillar of Delhi

Standing at the center of the Quwwatul Mosque the Iron Pillar is one of Delhi's most curious structures. Dating back to 4th century A.D., the pillar bears an inscription which states that it was erected as a flagstaff in honour of the Hindu god, Vishnu, and in the memory of the Gupta King Chandragupta II (375-413).

How the pillar moved to its present location remains a mystery. The pillar also highlights ancient India's achievements in metallurgy. The pillar is made of 98 per cent wrought iron and has stood 1,600 years without rusting or decomposing. Take the case of the Brahmi inscription alone. Readings of this six-line, three-stanza inscription in Sanskrit verse vary considerably, the one most often published being that by Fleet, who translated it in 1888.

It speaks, in very poetic terms, of the powerful, all-conquering monarch who had the pillar made: "He on whose arm fame was inscribed by the sword, when in battle in the Vanga countries, he kneaded (and turned) back with (his) breast the enemies who, uniting together, came against him; … he, by the breezes of whose prowess the southern ocean is even still perfumed."

But, this eloquent panegyric apart, when it comes to identifying the king with clarity, and giving further details about the erection of the pillar, the inscription suddenly leaves some questions unanswered: obviously, not for those who lived in those early times, but for later generations, for whom so much information was lost in the centuries that have gone by.

Thus, the verse concludes with the words: "He who, having the name of Chandra, carried a beauty of countenance like (the beauty of) the full moon, having in faith fixed his mind upon (the God) Vishnu, (had) this lofty standard of the divine Vishnu set up on the hill (called) Vishnupada."

But who exactly was King Chandra remains a puzzle.

On other grounds, historical or paleographic, it can be concluded that the pillar belongs to the Gupta period, but, from among the imperial Guptas, who is it that is referred to here simply by the name of 'Chandra': Chandragupta I, Chandragupta II, also celebrated as Vikramaditya, or, as some firmly believe, Samudragupta? Again, the Guptas were known to have been devotees of Lord Vishnu, but where was this hill called 'Vishnupada' located?

In a report published in the journal Current Science, R. Balasubramaniam of the IIT Kanpur explains how the pillar's resistance to corrosion is due to a passive protective film at the iron-rust interface. The presence of second-phase particles (slag and unreduced iron oxides) in the microstructure of the iron, that of high amounts of phosphorus in the metal, and the alternate wetting and drying existing under atmospheric conditions are the three main factors in the three-stage formation of that protective passive film.

Many theories have been put forward from time to time to explain the rust-free state of the pillar.

For example, the site of the pillar is away from industrial areas and the climate of Delhi is fairly dry.

It is known that serious corrosion of iron does not take place if critical value of relative humidity is less than 80%. At Delhi, the relative humidity exceeds 80% for only about 20 days in a year and exceeds 70% for only about 65 days in a year. Therefore, although the total rainfall annually is about 15-30 inches the atmosphere in Delhi is not very conducive to rusting of iron. Besides a dry environment, there appears to be no doubt that the protective scale on the pillar has played a major role in protecting this monument. There are two major theories of formation of this protective scale. It is quite possible that both the factors have played equally important roles in formation of this scale.

According to the second theory, the protective oxide could have formed from atmospheric exposure. Examination of small pieces of scale obtained from the iron pillar reveals that it consists of approximately 80% of an oxide of iron having the properties of the solid solution phase of mixtures of FeO and Fe_2O_3. About 10% of this hydrated oxide of iron, approaching Limonite ($Fe_2O_3.3H_2O$) has also been reported. From the above reports it can be concluded that the scale was apparently formed under conditions of heating with significant extent of atmospheric oxidation occurring at the surface and penetrating along cracks running longitudinally in the scale.

There have also been suggestions that the past pillar was ceremonially anointed with purified butter. Ghee obtained from the milk of cow would have had a marked effect. A thin coating of linseed oil or lanoline or wool grease is well known to give good protection to steel for some months. If applied regularly and reinforced b the dust and sand which settle on it, it gives a good protective coating to the material underneath. However, the practice of ceremonial anointing would probably have been discontinued during Muslim occupation of the area in 12th century AD.

So, in brief, it can be concluded that the corrosion resistance property of the Delhi Pillar is due to: (i) the purity of its iron; (ii) high phosphorus; (iii) low sulphur; (iv) absence of any other metal; (v) cinder coating formed on the surface; (vi) better forge welding; (vii) drier and uncontaminated atmospheric condition; and (viii) mass metal effect.

What exact processes were followed in forging it into shape at that early a point of time, the 4th/5th century AD? Above all, from the scientists' point of view, what is the secret, the great mystery, behind the fact of its being virtually non-rusting? There seems to be no end to the questions.

2012 PHENOMENA

- *Mayan Calendar*

- *Nibiru*

- *I Ching*

The Mayan Calendar

The Mayans were an advanced civilization who inhabited the Americas before the arrival of the Europeans. The civilization consisted of several indigenous but related tribes and collectively they created a civilization which was on par with that of Ancient Greece in field of scientific advancements made.

The Mayans had a special penchant for time keeping. They understood time as something sacred and believed it their duty to keep track of the days. The Mayans had developed three separate calendars for different purposes:

1. TZOLKIN: It was a 260-day calendar mend to keep track of religious ceremonies and other festivals.

2. HAAB': It was a 365-day solar calendar and kept track of ordinary days. It was very much like the calendar we use today.

3. LONG COUNT CALENDAR: It is this calendar which is so famous. The Mayans, it is believed, used this calendar to keep track of both the distant past and possibly, the 'future'.

Because the Mayans considered time as a cyclic phenomenon, all three calendars were created in a way that they reset themselves after a certain period. The first two – Tzolkin and Haab' – reset every 52 years but the Long Count Calendar reset after (roughly) 5,125 years and what has made this Long Count Calendar so famous is the fact that it is going to reset again on 21 December, 2012.

When the Europeans arrived on the American continent,

all but four Mayan books were burnt so it is hard to exactly find out what the Mayans themselves thought of the Long Count Calendar. However, it is has been interpreted, from the what little survives, that the Mayans believed that the Gods had destroyed three races of humans for not keeping track of time – Mayans themselves considered it a sacred duty – and considered themselves the fourth race.

The Mayan calendar dates back to August 11, 3114 BCE in Gregorian reckoning and entails two separate calendar cycles.

The religious belief system of the ancient Maya, which included cycles of creation and destruction, informed their concept of time. Many historians who have studied the Mayan calendar believe that it most likely began as a type of Farmers' Almanac or divinatory tool. The Maya saw time as both linear and cyclical and had two main calendar-like systems to map these different timeframes. Like the months and the year of the Gregorian calendar, the Mayan calendar was based upon the repetition of seasons and events in the cosmos. The Maya calculated time in two cycles, a short, cyclical cycle called the "Calendar Round," and a long, linear cycle called the "Long Count."

The shorter measure of time was calculated by a calendar cycle of fifty-two years, or 18,980 days, and was called the Calendar Round.

The Calendar Round was a combination of two smaller calendar measurements called the Sacred Round and Haab' cycles, which were used for the measurements of one's birthday as well as communal celebrations, religious festivals and agricultural cycles.

The longer phases of time were measured by the Long Count calendar.

The Long Count calendar is said to record the world's creation, even though the Mayans did not consider this to be the beginning of time. Each day of the Long Count has a unique number, commonly represented as five digits separated by periods, such as 1.2.4.9.11. Each number represents specific units of chronological measurement, largest to smallest, from left to right. The units are named baktun, katun, tun, winal, and kin. A baktun is equal to 144,000 days, a katun is 7,200 days, a tun is 360 days, a winal is 20 days, and kin is equal to a single day. The number of days indicated by the five digits is equal to the number of days since the Mayans believed the world was created.

The Mayans also recorded celestial movements, such as lunar phases, the rising and setting of the sun, and lunar cycles. The Mayans believed that all planets, the moon, and the sun were divine. In addition, the cycles of the planet Venus were recorded, as this planet was thought to be the bearer of bad luck and war. They also watched and recorded the thirteen constellations of the zodiac. The Mayan calendar and other Mayan cosmic recording systems are extremely intricate.

Through mathematical calculations, astronomers and scholars have been able to convert the dates of the Long Count calendar to those of the Gregorian calendar. Scholars generally agree that the beginning date of the Mayan calendar is August 11, 3114 BCE; according to Mayan belief, this date marks the creation of the world. In Mayan inscription, this date is represented as 13.0.0.0.0, where the thirteen serves as a zero. According to the Mayan mathematical system, the calendar covers a span of time that is 13 baktun, or 187,200 days. At the end of the time span of 187,200 days, the calendar dating system will once again read 13.0.0.0.0.

According to Mayan belief, this date will be the

anniversary of the creation of the world, and a cycle of creation and destruction will have been completed. The parallel Gregorian calendar date is December 21, 2012, which also represents the winter solstice. However, unlike the popular beliefs of the end of the world surrounding the 2012 phenomenon, the Mayans never had an explicit prophecy regarding what would happen when the calendar ended.

Those who find significance in the end of the current long-count cycle hold numerous theories and predictions regarding the date December 21, 2012. Speculations today include the end of the world, extraordinary cosmic events, world peace, and more.

Others have interpreted the end of the long-count cycle of the Mayan calendar through the lens of their own religious belief system. Still others have made speculations regarding astronomical occurrences including a rare alignment of all the planets which will be the cause of numerous, destructive, outcomes, though astronomers have confirmed that the alignment of such planets on December 21, 2012 will not happen.

Nibiru

In 1976, the late Zecharia Sitchin stirred up a great deal of controversy with the publication of his book, The Twelfth Planet. In this and subsequent books, Sitchin presented his literal translations of ancient Sumerian texts which told an incredible story about the origins of humankind on planet Earth.

The ancient cuneiform texts -- some of the earliest known writing, dating back some 6,000 years -- told the story of a race of beings called the Anunnaki.

The Anunnaki came to Earth from a planet in our solar system called Nibiru, according to the Sumerians via Sitchin.

Nibiru's orbit around the Sun is highly elliptical, according to Sitchin's books, taking it out beyond the orbit of Pluto at its farthest point and bringing it as close to the Sun as the far side of the asteroid belt (a ring of asteroids that is known to occupy a band of space between the orbits of Mars and Jupiter). It takes Nibiru 3,600 years to complete one orbital journey, and it was last in this vicinity around 160 B.C.E. The gravitational effects of a sizable planet moving close to the inner solar system, as it is claimed for Nibiru, could wreak havoc on the orbits of other planets, disrupt the asteroid belt and spell big trouble for planet Earth.

Now going back to Annunaki.

The most astonishing fact that Sumerian text revealed is that how Homo sapiens were created by Annunaki with the help of his associates. Sitchin's translation says that Annunaki came to our planet approximately 450,000 years ago in order to mine gold in a place in present day's Zimbabwe.

A recent research by an Anglo-American corp. has confirmed that an extensive scale of gold mining in the same area, at least 100,000 years ago. All the mined gold used to shipped back to Annunaki's planet, and the workers used to work in mines was from his planet too. After a rebellion Annunaki decided to create a new working class to do the mining for them-probably this is the very first concept of enslavement of human race in our entire history.

In order to create a new slave or working class for mining work, the Annunaki's genes and the native human genes were mixed up in a test tube to create the new race- Homo sapiens. This really sounds like a fairy tale, yet our modern science says us that around 200,000 years back there was a sudden change or upgrade of human form-famously known as the missing link.

It is believed that Annunaki inter breeded with Earth races in order to create a more adaptive race with the earth atmosphere and to rule the planet with full control. During the time of summers (4000-5000 BC), in a place in modern day Iraq, God was depicted as human like form, but before that in Ubaid culture, in the same area in Iraq, God was depicted as reptilian-humanoids.

Why there would be a sudden change in depiction of God in the same place within a short period of time- is not known to us so far. But there are many accounts about the human inter-breeding with the extra-terrestrials and Sumerian tablets are the most ancient source of information about God, inter-breeding, and extra-terrestrial intervention in creation of human race.

They seem to belong to planet X or Nibiru.

Going back to Nibiru:

This anomalous body was first spotted in 1983 by IRAS (InfraredAstronomical Satellite), according to news stories. The Washington Post reported: "A heavenly body possibly as large as the giant planet Jupiter and possibly so close to Earth that it would be part of this solar system has been found in the direction of the constellation Orion by an orbiting telescopeaboard the U.S. infrared astronomical satellite. So mysterious is the object that astronomers do not know if it is a planet, a giant comet, a nearby 'protostar' that never got hot enough to become a star, a distant galaxy so young that it is still in the process of forming its first stars or a galaxy so shrouded in dust that none of the light cast by its stars ever gets through."

Nibiru supporters contend that IRAS has, in fact, spotted the wandering planet.

Some of the Nibiru researchers also cite the prophecies of Edgar Cayce who predicted that we would soon suffer monumental Earth changes and a pole shift, even though he did not attribute them to anything as specific as a visiting planet. And, of course, the much-analyzed Mayan calendar is said to set the "end of world" in December, 2012.

They claim, Nibiru to be round the corner and once we are able to see it. Great Doom will befall us. Annunaki is presently visiting us as our time supposedly is over.

But if they do exist, why don't we see them or are they really mixed up with human and are much more intelligent than us-only time will tell us the true story.

STRANGEST MYSTERIES OF THE WORLD AND BEYOND

I Ching and 2012

The relation between the I Ching and 2012 is publicized in a book called "The Invisible Landscape: Mind, Hallucinogens, and the I Ching" written by Terence McKenna who died in 2000.

In his book, he was inspired by the 64 Hexagram arrangements in King Wen's I Ching (Book of Change).

In the I Ching, King Wen has a special sequence in arranging the order of the 64 hexagrams, putting them in the order with Heaven (The Creative) and Earth (The Receptive) as first and second Hexgram, after going through 60 hexagrams arranged in 30 pairs, it ends with the final pairs Water on Fire (After Completion) and Fire on Water (Before Completion). This sequence is taken to represent different stage of development of the world from the beginning with Heaven and Earth to the end with Fire on Water.

Inspired by this sequence, McKenna assigned mathematical values to each of 384 lines (jao) of the 64 hexagram and he came up with a curve which he claimed is reflecting the timing of important world events. Every peak and bottom point of the curve seems co inside with an important stage in human civilization. He called this a Time Wave theory, and it seems if one translate the 384 lines of King Wen's 64 Hexagrams into time, according to this theory, we will find the time interval between big events on earth.

His most significant theory is that if he put the end date of the curve at 21/12/2012, then all the peak and bottom points of his curve match with significant events in human history. Hence, he considers the date 21/12/2012 is the ending day when the curve reaches the bottom.

As such, the I Ching itself actually did not predict 2012, at best, one can only say it gives inspiration to McKenna to invent the Time wave theory. The original meaning of the last two Hexagrams – After Completion and Before Completion does not imply end of the world, to the contrary, it implies there is no ending, because the change is not yet completed. It is like many cyclical changes in nature, when one year's four season finished, another new year's four season begins. So, it is wrong and not fair to say the 2012 doomsday is predicted by I Ching.

Is there anything in the I Ching that can be associated with such end of world ideas?

The most relevant could be the "Supreme World Order principles" invented by Shao Yong of Sung Dynasty. Shao Yong is an expert of I Ching and he invented a time counting system dividing time into Yuan, Huai, Yun, Shi.

10,000 years ago, humans began domesticating plants and animals.

500 years ago, we invented the printing press.

100 years ago, we began driving automobiles.

50 years ago, we invented the computer.

30 years ago, we landed on the moon.

The speed of change is rapid. Population, computing power, speed of transport, the sheer amount of known information, and most other things that involve humans, are all increasing at an accelerating rate.

Maybe there will come a time when the rate of change will

reach such a speed that change is all that will exist. Various fringe scientists have tried to calculate this point of infinity, giving us calculated dates ranging from 2010 to 2050. Dates that many of us will live to see. Perhaps the date is Dec 22, 2012.

About what may happen in 2012 they have this to say:

"Achievement of the zero state can be imagined to arrive in one of two forms. One is the dissolution of the cosmos in an actual cessation and unraveling of the natural laws, a literal apocalypse. The other possibility... the culmination of a human process, a process of tool making, which comes to completion in the perfect artifact: the monadic self, exteriorised, condensed, and visible in three dimensions; in alchemical terms, the dream of a union of spirit and matter."

In the end, I would say. What is your interpretation?

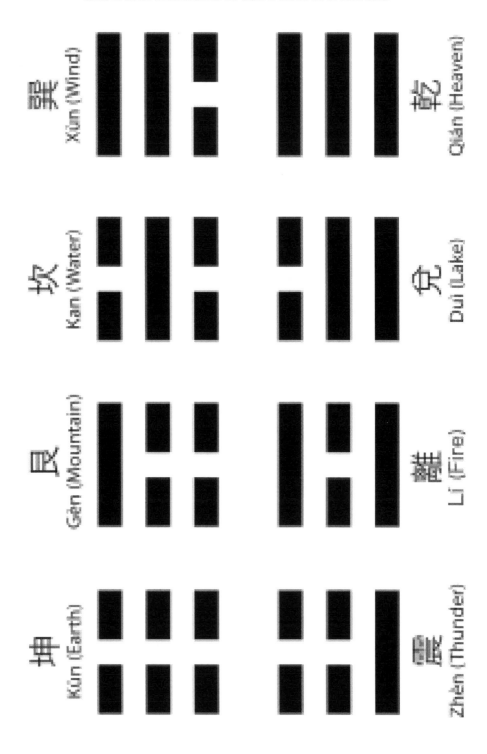

MONSTERS

- *Loch Ness Monster*

- *Yeti*

Loch Ness Monster

Loch Ness is located in the North of Scotland and is one of a series of interlinked lochs which run along the Great Glen. The Great Glen is a distinctive incision which runs across the country and represents a large geological fault zone. The interlinking was completed in the 19th century following the completion of the Caledonian Canal.

Loch Ness, the largest freshwater lake in the British Isles, is twenty-four miles long and, at one point, one and a half miles wide. It has an average depth of four hundred and fifty feet and at times plunges close to a thousand. It is cold and murky, with dangerous currents. In short, it is the perfect place to hide a monster from even the most prying eyes of science.

Many bodies of water in Northern Scotland have ancient legends about monsters that were never written down.

A tale that supposedly occurred in 565 A.D. tells of Saint Columba who saved a swimmer from a hungry monster in the Ness river. This story was recorded in the book The Life of Saint Columba sometime in the late 7th Century and is often connected with later sightings in the nearby lake.

In 1933, after a new road was built along the edge of the Loch, the number of reports soared. The first of these came on April 14 when the owners of an inn in Drumnadrochit, the Mackays, observed an "enormous animal "rolling and plunging" in the Loch. They reported it to Alex Campbel, the man in charge of regulating salmon fishing in the Loch. Campbel spent a lot of time at the lake and observed the monster himself several times after being told of the Mackay sighting.

Campbel described the creature as having "a long, tapering neck, about 6 feet long, and a smallish head with a serpentine look about it, and a huge hump behind..." Campbel estimated the length of the "monster" to be about thirty feet.

The first photograph of the thing was taken in 1933 by Hugh Gray. Gray reported, "I immediately got my camera ready and snapped the object which was then two to three feet above the surface of the water. I did not see any head, for what I took to be the front parts were under the water, but there was considerable movement from what seemed to be the tail."

Probably the most famous picture of the Loch Ness monster was the "surgeon's photo" supposedly taken by Colonel Robert Wilson in 1934. It shows a long, thin neck rising above the water connected to a hump-like body. This photo is thought to be a fake, though, after the confession of Christian Spurling who helped build the model monster that was photographed. He admitted the hoax shortly before he died in 1993 at age 90.

Early in 1934 there was a land sighting of the beast. Arthur Grant, a young veterinary student, was out on his motorcycle one evening when he almost ran into the monster as it crossed the road. Grant's description of the thing, small head, long tapering neck and tail with a bulky body and flippers, seemed to match the appearance of the plesiosaurus. The plesiosaurus, an aquatic, reptilian contemporary of the dinosaurs, was thought to have been extinct for at least 65 million years.

In April of 1960, Tim Dinsdale, while visiting the lake, captured the first moving picture of the monster. Though the film shows little, a group of Royal Air Force photographic experts pronounced that the object was "probably" animate and as long as ninety feet. Skeptics argued that the thing was probably a motorboat. Dinsdale was convinced enough by his own pictures to give up his career as an aeronautical engineer and devote the next twenty years of his life to finding the monster. Though Dinsdale was rewarded with two more sightings of the creature, he was never able to gather incontrovertible proof of its existence.

The next major event for Nessie was a study of the Loch Monster started in 1970 by the American Academy of Applied Science. The group, headed by Dr. Robert Rines, used automatic cameras and sonar to monitor the Loch. In 1972 one of the underwater cameras got four frames of what appeared to be a flipper six to eight feet long.

One-night Peter Davies, a member of Rines' team, was out in a small boat in the Loch when he had a close encounter with the beast. He detected it under his boat with sonar. "I don't mind telling you it was a rather strange feeling," said Davies, "rowing across that pitch-black water knowing that there was a very large animal just thirty feet below. It was the sheer size of the echo trace that was frightening."

Though the photograph most often seen by the public seems to clearly show something that looks like the diamond-shaped fin of a plesiosaurus, some photographic experts have argued that the image has been retouched. In the original images the interpretation is much more ambiguous.

In 1975 one of the team's cameras captured a vague and fuzzy image that could be interpreted as the face of the beast. "I thought that would clinch it," remarked Rines," but as you know, it didn't at all." The photograph, known as the "gargoyle head," was identified by a later expedition as the remains of a tree stump.

Various researchers have employed sonar to find the

monster with varying results. In 1968 professor DG Tucker of the University of Birmingham tested a prototype sonar at the Loch. The transducer was mounted at one side of the lake, pointing at the opposite side so that any objects passing through its beam would be detected. During a two-week period, multiple animate objects 20 feet in length were detected moving up and down from the loch bottom to midwater, but never surfacing. The size and movement did not seem to match that of any known fish. Tucker even declared, "The high rate of ascent and descent makes it seem very unlikely that they could be fish, and fishery biologists we have consulted cannot suggest what fish they might be. It is a temptation to suppose they might be the fabulous Loch Ness monsters, now observed for the first time in their underwater activities!"

A year later Andrew Carroll, a researcher for the New York Aquarium used sonar from his research launch Rangitea to sweep the Loch and picked up a strong echo of an animate object estimated to be twenty feet in length. Neither object found by Carroll or by Tucker were ever definitely identified.

Roy Mackal, a biologist at the University of Chicago who was interested in crypto zoology, built a system of underwater microphones and placed them in the loch to see if he could detect any sounds the monster might make. "Bird-like chirps", "knocks" and "clicks" were recorded along with a swishing sound which Mackal thought might be the sounds of an animal echolocation to find and hunt its prey. Mackal noted that the sounds stopped whenever a boat passed by and resumed after it had reached a safe distance.

The most recent sonar exploration of the Loch was in 2004 when an expedition from the BBC used 600 sonar beams to probe the Loch from end-to-end. They could detect no sign of a large living animal in its waters. Efforts have continued to find the monster. A small submarine was even used to explore the depths of the lake, but no convincing evidence was found.

Unfortunately, the history of the Loch Ness monster is filled with people creating hoaxes. In 1933, Marmaduke Wetherell, who himself was thought to be responsible for the famous Surgeon's Photo hoax, was himself hoaxed when he found the footprint of a large animal in the mud along the shore of Loch Ness. The mark was created using a dried hippo foot that was probably part of an umbrella stand. The incident, reported in the Daily Mail, humiliated Wetherell, who later got his revenge when his fake "Surgeon's Photo" appeared in that same publication.

One of the clearest photos of the Loch Ness monster was taken by Anthony 'Doc' Shiels in May of 1977. The picture is so clear; however, it immediately makes experts skeptical and has been referred to in some circles as "the Loch Ness Muppet." Shiels himself, a self-styled physic, has said that while he definitely takes photos of lake monsters, he doesn't believe in them.

As recently as March, 2005, two American students visiting the Loch claimed to have found a gigantic tooth stuck in the carcass of a deer. However, the object was actually the antler of a roe muntjac deer, not a Nessie fang. The whole story turned out to be a marketing ploy for an upcoming horror novel entitled The Loch, written by author Steve Alten.

Nessie has entered popular culture and is a symbol recognized around the world. In addition to appearing in Alten's book, Nessie has been featured in many films. This includes appearances as dangerous killer in The Loch Ness Horror (though in reality nobody has ever claimed they have been injured by the creatures), a secret submarine in the film The Private Life of Sherlock Holmes and, most recently, a child's magical friend in The Water Horse: Legend of the Deep.

If the monster truly exists and is not a hoax or a publicity stunt, it is extremely elusive. No bones or remains have ever been, found and short of draining the Loch, it seems impossible to disprove the existence of the creature.

Only Time will tell (not talking about Jeffrey Archer's novel).

Yeti

The Yeti is a kind of abominable snowman that looks like an ape. It belongs to the class of Cryptids, which are creatures that are believed to exist but scientifically, their existence is not confirmed. The most known features of Yeti, which have been known by people are that, it can walk like a man and has long white hairs covereing its whole body. It has a big man like foot which is a major evidence of it existence because many large, man like foot prints have been seen by people in its suppose habitat.

Where Does Yeti Live?

The popular place where the sightings of Yeti have been claimed is the Himalayas. The dangerous and extreme mountainous areas of the Himalayan region is a place where only a handful of local population have been living for centuries. Most of the people that come to this place arrive here for the purpose of mountaineering and hiking. So the reports about its sightings have been mostly registered by these mountaineers who saw its foot prints on high areas of Himalayas. Although many sightings have been reported yet, no one has really witnessed it up close to provide any sufficient evidence about its existence.

Bigfoot and Yeti

There is a close resemblance between existence of the Yeti and the American Bigfoot. The Bigfoot is a similar creature or a cryptid that is believed to live in the North-West region of America. Its main habitat is the forest area of North America. Similar stories like that of the Yeti, have been heard about Bigfoot.

The resemblance between these two cryptids is based on their similar appearance. With long hairy bodies and the common stories of their sighting, both these creatures resemble in their supposed appearance. Although it has been reported that the color of the Bigfoot is somewhat dark brownish as compared to white color of the Yeti.

Yeti Sightings

There has been many events of its sightings and most of them being mentioned in travel accounts of some adventurer. The first stories about Yeti's sightings emerged in the early 19th century when and adventurer B.H Hodgson claimed to have seen a long ape like creature who ran away on seeing his team.

Similar accounts were published about its sightings and man like foot trail, in the late 19th century.

Later in the 20th century when many mountaineers started to move to the Himalayan region, the number of sightings dramatically increased. The most popular of these is one by Eric Shipton in 1951. Eric even took some snaps of the Yeti while his visit but still it was thought to be an inconclusive evidence.

Even Sir Edmund Hillary reported footprints of Yeti during his famous Mount Everest expedition. Soon afterwards many new things started to appear like, hair samples of Yeti, Yeti's feces etc. Many researches were carried out on these specimens and some concluded them to be of something unknown while others related them to some bear or goat specie. This once again made everything inconclusive.

Present Sightings

Presently similar beliefs are being circulated about its

existence and recently the most authentic study about them was carried by a BBC team who analyzed a hair sample of Yeti. The hair after DNA test revealed its resemblance to that found by Sir Edmund Hillary during his expedition. A close analysis showed that these hairs belonged to the Himalayan Gorals.

Currently more stories are appearing on the scene and recently a Japanese team claimed to have filmed Yeti on their cameras. Such things continue to trouble scientists and it is really hard to find the authenticity of any of these claims.

So far there is no firm evidence to support the existence of the Yeti, but there is no way show that he doesn't exist either. If he indeed lives in the barren, frozen, upper reaches of the Himalayas where few men dare to tread, he may find his refuge safe for a long time to come.

ANCIENT MYSTERIES

- Baghdad Battery

- Abydos- Carvings of Futuristic Machines

- The Baigong Pipes

- Antikythera Mechanism- Oldest Computer of the World

Baghdad Battery

We all have heard of batteries. Today batteries can be found in any grocery, drug, convenience and department store you come across. Well, here's a battery that's 2,000 years old! (Astounding, isn't it?)

What is this battery?

Known as the Baghdad Battery.

In 1936, while excavating ruins of a 2000-year-old village near Baghdad, workers discovered mysterious small vase. A 6-inch-high pot of bright yellow clay dating back two millennia contained a cylinder of sheet-copper 5 inches by 1.5 inches. The edge of the copper cylinder was soldered with a 60-40 lead-tin alloy comparable to today's solder. The bottom of the cylinder was capped with a crimped-in copper disk and sealed with bitumen or asphalt. Another insulating layer of asphalt sealed the top and also held in place an iron rod suspended into the center of the copper cylinder. The rod showed evidence of having been corroded with an acidic agent.

According to most texts the "Voltic pile," or electric battery, was invented in 1800 by the Count Alassandro Volta. Volta had observed that when two dissimilar metal probes were placed against frog tissue, a weak electric current was generated. Volta discovered he could reproduce this current outside of living tissue by placing the metals in certain chemical solutions. For this, and his other work with electricity, we commemorate his name in the measurement of electric potential called the volt.

The little jar in Baghdad suggests that Volta didn't invent the battery, but reinvented it. The jar was first described by German archaeologist Wilhelm Konig in 1938. It is unclear if Konig dug the object up himself or located it within the holdings of the museum, but it is known that it was found, with several others, at a place called Khujut Rabu, just outside Baghdad.

The jars are believed to be about 2,000 years old and consist of an earthenware shell, with a stopper composed of asphalt. Sticking through the top of the stopper is an iron rod. Inside the jar the rod is surrounded by a cylinder of copper. Konig thought these things looked like electric batteries and published a paper on the subject in 1940.

World War II prevented immediate follow-up on the jars, but after hostilities ceased, an American, Willard F. M. Gray of the General Electric High Voltage Laboratory in Pittsfield, Massachusetts, built some reproductions. When filled with an electrolyte like grape juice, the devices produced about two volts.

If they were batteries, though, who made them and what were they used for? Right, I mean this is definitely the foremost question.

It is said, Khujut Rabu was a settlement of a people called the Parthians. While the Parthians were excellent fighters, they had not been noted for their technological achievements and some researchers have suggested they obtained the batteries from someone else. A few people have even suggested that this someone else was a space traveler that visited Earth during ancient times.

As romantic a notion as this is, there is nothing about the Baghdad batteries that is high-tech. All the materials used are common in origin and the manufacture was well within the ability of many of the peoples of that era. What is surprising about the jars is that somebody figured out how to put the right materials together in the right way to make a device that has a function which was not obvious. It is likely that the batteries (if that is what they are) the result of an isolated and accidental development.

It more seems like a chain of events.

It is suggested that they were used to electroplate items (a feat recently duplicated on the show Discovery Channel show MythBusters). The electroplating process uses a small electric current to put a thin layer of one metal (such as gold) on to the surface of another (such as silver).

This idea is appealing because at its core lies the mother of many inventions: money.

In the making of jewellery, for example, a layer of gold or silver is often applied to enhance its beauty in a process called gilding.

Also, some have suggested the batteries may have been used medicinally.

The ancient Greeks wrote of the pain killing effect of electric fish when applied to the soles of the feet.

The Chinese had developed acupuncture by this time, and still use acupuncture combined with an electric current. This may explain the presence of needle-like objects found with some of the batteries.

But this tiny voltage would surely have been ineffective against real pain, considering the well-recorded use of other painkillers in the ancient world like cannabis, opium and wine.

Or was it used in Magical rituals:

It is said that to the uninitiated, science cannot be distinguished from magic. "In Egypt we know this sort of thing happened with Hero's engine," Dr Craddock says.

Hero's engine was a primitive steam-driven machine, and like the battery of Baghdad, no one is quite sure what it was used for, but are convinced it could work.

If this idol could be found, it would be strong evidence to support the new theory. With the batteries inside, was this object once revered, like the Oracle of Delphi in Greece, and "charged" with godly powers?

Even if the current were insufficient to provide a genuine shock, it may have felt warm, a bizarre tingle to the touch of the unsuspecting finger. (Quite an enigma)

At the very least, it could have just been the container of these articles, to keep their secret safe.

Perhaps it is too early to say the battery has been convincingly demonstrated to be part of a magical ritual. Further examination, including accurate dating, of the batteries' components are needed to really answer this mystery.

Where can we see this battery? If we want to, where is it placed?

They have been placed in the Baghdad Museum, with others which were unearthed in Iraq, all dated from the Parthian occupation between 248 BCE and 226 CE.

Definitely, a worthwhile visit,eh!

Abydos- Carvings of Futuristic Machines

In 1848, an archaeological expedition working in Egypt discovered strange hieroglyphs on a ceiling beam at an ancient temple in Abydos, located approximately 450 kilometers south of Cairo in Egypt. The hieroglyphs were carefully copied and brought back to Europe. The mysterious images gave rise to heated debate amongst Egyptologists.

They found a series of carvings that look very much like helicopters and futuristic space craft. The Helicopter is particularly recognizable and this has led to questions being raised about how this can possibly exist.

Eventually, however, they were dismissed as bizarre objects that nobody could adequately explain and were forgotten.

In the mid 1990's photographs and videos, taken primarily by tourists who had visited Abydos, began to appear on the internet. They depicted the 'strange machine hieroglyphs' originally discovered in the nineteenth century. The temple in which they were found was built by Pharaoh Seti I around three thousand years ago.

To the modern viewer it is clear that the strange machines, so mysterious to the Victorians, are in fact various types of flying craft and a tank. One of the aircraft is a helicopter. There is no mistaking it. It has a rotor blade, cockpit and tailfin typical of a modern battle helicopter. On the face of it, this is one of the most astounding discoveries ever to have been made in Egypt.

The respected Arab newspaper 'Al-Sharq Al-Awsat' published several photographs taken at another Egyptian temple, the Amon Ra Temple in Karnak.

The photographs are of carvings believed to be three thousand years old. They appear very similar to the carvings found at Abydos. There is a battle helicopter with a distinct rotor and a tail unit, and nearby, other modern-looking flying craft. So, there are in fact not one, but two almost identical sets of carvings at Karnak and Abydos. What are the chances of that being due to identical palimpsest effects at both locations?

So, accepting the fact that the ancient Egyptians did not have the technology to build helicopters or other aircraft, where did the images of the flying machines come from? The history of the human race has been turbulent to say the least. Many of the fabulous ancient libraries, such as the library at Alexandria and the vast libraries of ancient China have been destroyed. Much of the priceless evidence of the distant past has been obliterated. Fortunately, however, ancient writings have survived, particularly in India. Amazingly, some of these ancient texts speak of highly sophisticated flying craft.

It was reported that the Chinese have discovered extremely old Sanskrit documents in Tibet and sent them to the University of Chandigarh in India to be translated. Apparently, the documents contain instructions for building spacecraft. Surprisingly, the Chinese announced that they were evaluating this ancient technology for potential inclusion in their space program!

There is increasing evidence that the so-called 'Rama Empire' of Northern India and Pakistan is far more ancient than had been originally supposed. Remnants of its large sophisticated cities are still to be found in the deserts of Pakistan, and in Northern and Western India. According to ancient Indian texts, the Empire of Rama had flying machines which were called 'Vimanas'. The texts on Vimanas are numerous, and highly detailed. The ancient Indians wrote entire flight manuals on the control of the various types of Vimanas, many of which are still in existence; some have now been translated into English. Different types of Vimanas were described; some were saucer shaped, others cigar shaped. The Vimanas appeared to be powered by some sort of anti-gravity device, as they took off vertically and were capable of hovering in the air.

The compelling temple carvings at Abydos and Karnak, and ancient texts from India and Tibet, speak of a bygone era when powered flight was highly advanced and even commonplace. They speak of a long-lost civilization that was at least as advanced as our own. It was not a civilization that existed three thousand years ago, but much further back in the mists of time; a civilization that was suddenly wiped from the face of the Earth. Did they whiz around in strange futuristic craft or did they just witness something they couldn't explain and carve it in stone as a record. Perhaps time will tell but it hasn't so far.

The Baigong Pipes

Ancient plumbers, anyone?

Local legend speculates that Mt. Baigong in the Qinghai Province of China is an ancient extraterrestrial laboratory.

In rural China, in a location that is considered to be uninhabitable to humans, there are three openings in Mount Baigong that contain hundreds of rustic iron pipes. Some of the pipes run deep into the mountain, others run to a nearby lake. There are more pipes in the lake bottom and there are pipes scattered along the shoreline. The pipes are cleanly cut and not jagged, so they appear to have had a use at one time. This all seems mundane: some pipes sticking out of the ground in China, but archeologists dated the pipes to a time when humanity was just getting familiar with fire, making casting iron impossible.

Some ufologists think that the pipes were part of some sort of UFO landing site or alien complex. They cite that the pipes contain silica, which is also found on Mars, as evidence, but it is important to note that silica can be found in lots of cast iron materials.

The first scientists to examine the subterranean phenomenon concluded that the pipes were composed of 92% common minerals and metals and 8% unknown materials. The obvious inference is that these red-hued tubes were transported here from outer space as part of an alien public works project.

This Martian theory has garnered so much support that a monument topped off with a corroded satellite dish has been erected near the mountain.

The most recent researchers to examine the pipes believe that the metallic phenomena are in fact fossilized tree root casts, the rusted tubes being the result of tree roots that underwent the processes of pedogenesis (the process that forms soils) and diagenesis (transformation of soil into rock). Further experiments confirmed that the pipes contain organic plant material and even microscopic tree rings. Overflow from an extinct lake once carried these roots to where they stand now.

What purpose did these pipes serve and who put them there?

Many have simply written off the Baigong pipes as a hoax, but doing this ignores the fact that the iron pipes date back to over 5,000 years ago.

Gosh! How do you explain that?

The Antikythera Mechanism - Oldest Computer of the World

A very mysterious object that turned history upside down is the so-called Antikythera Mechanism.

In 1900 a sponge diver was working in the Mediterranean, just off the island of Antikythera at a depth of about 138 feet. Divers had noticed various fragments of ancient cargo scattered along the bottom of this location but it was one Elias Stadaitos who discovered the source of these artifacts.

Elias found the remains of a Roman cargo ship and for many months he returned to the site to find statues, pottery and interesting clumps of rock which often encrusted metallic objects.

In May of 1902 an archaeologist named Valerios Stais noticed that one piece of interesting rock seemed to have what looked like a gear wheel embedded in it and set the piece aside for further inspection.

The original piece of rock was about 13 inches high, 7 inches wide and only 3 inches thick, leading many to speculate that it was probably just a piece of a much larger mechanism. There were also symbols etched in the metal which later were shown to be Greek.

Although difficult to date, the strange artifact was thought to be over two thousand years old, making it one of the earliest precision geared devices in existence. The fine teeth of the gears suggested it was some type of clock mechanism, but the complexity of the pieces also suggested that it was designed to do more than tell the time of day.

The artifact, which became known as "the Antikythera Mechanism" was largely unknown for many decades as it was meticulously cleaned. In 1951 when the encrusted rock had finally been cleared to reveal the badly eroded gears, a British scientist named Derek Price began a comprehensive study of the devices function and probably use.

What makes it so mysterious is that the mechanical technology, and the purpose of the object, is typical of 18th century technology – not BC technology!

All the metal parts of the machine seem to have been cut from a single sheet of low-tin bronze about two millimeters thick; no parts were cast or made of a different metal. From the ancient Greek inscriptions on the plate of the clock, we can assume that it dates from the first century BC.

It was designed for use in astronomy and served to calculate sunrise, sunset and moon movements. This all means that more than 2000 years ago, the Greeks – or someone who expressed himself in the old-Greek language – were already using technology which we only invented 300 years ago.

The Antikythera Mechanism gained world attention when it was the cover story in Scientific American (June 1959) and was later exposed to the general public by Arthur Clarke's book Mysterious World.

In Clarke's book he described the mechanism as "The world's first computer" and suggested that it was capable of calculating the position of the stars and planets.

This was largely disputed by historians who reminded the world that "planets" were only a vague concept of scholars around the time of Copernicus in the sixteenth century!

Although the mechanism has been cleaned, many of the gears were believed to remain encrusted and corroded in the remaining stone. To chip away at this stone would certainly destroy any traces of the gears that remained. Scientists looked for other methods to "see" inside the remaining rock and to determine the full extent of the gears.

In 1971, Price joined forces with Charalampos Kararalos, professor of nuclear physics at the Greek National Center of Scientific Research and devised a way to x-ray the rock with powerful gamma rays.

Their experiment was very successful and revealed additional gears which were critical in understanding how the mechanism functioned.

Scientists from around the globe were surprised at the miniaturization of the gears - similar to work of fine watchmakers centuries later!

It was also highly complex, suggesting that the fundamental knowledge of mechanics was well advanced.

Although the device was analog (mechanical) it could calculate with the accuracy of a slide rule. It plotted angular velocities, the synodic and sideral lunar cycles, and presented the position of the known planets and moon for any date entered.

Aside from being an engineering mystery, the device showed that the designers understood that the sun was the center of the local system - not the Earth.

This view would later be worthy of imprisonment or even death by the geocentric Roman Catholics of later centuries.

The fragments show that the original instrument carried at least four large areas of inscription: outside the front door, inside the back door, on the plate between the two back dials and on the parapegma plates near the front dial.

The main inscriptions are in a sorry state and only short snatches of them can be read. To provide an idea of their condition it need only be said that in some cases a plate has completely disappeared, leaving behind an impression of its letters, standing up in a mirror image, in relief on the soft corrosion products on the plate below.

It is remarkable that such inscriptions can be read at all.

But even from the evidence of a few complete words one can get an idea of the subject matter.

**The sun is mentioned several times, and the planet Venus once

**Terms are used that refer to the stations and retro gradations of planets

**The ecliptic is named

**Pointers, apparently those of the dials, are mentioned

**A line of one inscription significantly records "76 years, 19 years"

(This refers to the well-known Calippic cycle of 76 years, which is four times the Metonic cycle of 19 years, or 235 synodic (lunar) months)

**The next line includes the number "223," which refers to the eclipse cycle of 223 lunar months

Putting together the information gathered so far, it seems

reasonable to suppose that the whole purpose of the Antikythera device was to mechanize just this sort of cyclical relation, which was a strong feature of ancient astronomy.

Other functions provided by this device were described as:

**A 365-day calendar which favored in a leap year every four years

**Prediction of solar and lunar eclipses

**A star almanac which showed when various constellations of the Greek zodiac would move across the sky+

Definitely, a wonder machine?!

FASCINATING PLACES

- Fly Geyser

- Pamukkale

- The Door to Hell

- The Principality of Sealand: The World's Smallest Country

- Racetrack Playa

Fly Geyser

Heard of a geyser that lies on a private property and grows in size.

Yes, the fly Geyser!

This mysterious natural phenomenon has indeed a look of a place which is more familiar to some scene from sci-fi movies rather than the nature we are used to see. And what makes it even more mysterious is that this geyser is located on private ranch which is owned by a person who does not want to allow the close public access to the place.

This weird fly geyser can be found in Hualapai Valley near Gerlach in Nevada. It "made itself" during the 1960s by all the water and minerals that is their content. Around the geyser small fishes live in the pounds, as well as swans and mallards. This fly geyser is 4 meters high and is built by many years of minerals just piling around it.

Despite its unusual shape, of three lions which are furiously spitting the water, the location isn't actually much known, even amongst the residents in the nearby towns and places, probably because the private owner is keeping this true treasure only for himself.

The Fly Geyser, near Gerlach, Nevada, is strange because it somehow grows up. It is three meters high at the moment.

Wish the owner Bill Spoo will let tourists flock in. It is definitely a wondrous natural phenomenon.

Pamukkale

Ever been to the 'Cotton Castle'?

Pamukkale, meaning "cotton castle" in Turkish, is a natural site in Denizli Province in southwestern Turkey. The city contains hot springs and travertines, terraces of carbonate minerals left by the flowing water. It is located in Turkey's Inner Aegean region, in the River Menderes valley, which has a temperate climate for most of the year.

According to the legend that spread the mystery of Hierapolis to the wide world, an ugly shepherd girl, fed up with the burdens of life, cast herself into water, but turned into a beautiful maiden in the waters of Hierapolis.

Hierapolis was founded during the Phrygian era, and its name was derived from Hiera, the beautiful wife of Telephos, the King of Pergamon. Hierapolis played an important role in spreading Christianity in Asia Minor, and it was the place where Phillip, one of the twelve Apostles of Jesus Christ, died. For this reason, Hierapolis became an important religious centre in the 4th century AD. Later it assumed the title of the Guide of the East and saw its most brilliant years between 96 and 162 AD. Hierapolis came under Byzantine rule in 395, and became a metropolitan bishopric.

History and nature meet in an extraordinary manner at Pamukkale. (Check the photograph on your right. Truly, Beautiful!)

The Pamukkale travertine was created by thermal water depositing the calcium carbonate it contained. The natural wonder of Pamukkale travertine deposits span a 160 meters tall and 2700 meters long cascade. With its brilliant white color, it can be seen about a distance of 20 km. At Pamukkale there are 17 thermal springs with water temperatures between 35-100-C.

The thermal mineral water springs and exceptional scenery have impressed people since antiquity. Wealthy people came from Rome and other cities of Anatolia to spend their last years in Hierapolis. Because of this, the Necropolis (the grave yard) is full of monumental tombs decorated in the styles of different regions.

The white surroundings just lend an aura of exquisiteness to the area.

The Door to Hell

"The Door to Hell" is more than a scene out of a movie, it's a giant flaming hole in the middle of the Karakum Desert that has been burning for 40 years.

The long burning crater is located in the middle of the Karakum Desert in Derweze, Turkmenistan.

While Biblical alarmists might point to the "Door of Hell" as yet another sign of a coming apocalypse, but it definitely has a scientific explanation. Soviet geologists were drilling at the site in 1971 and tapped into a cavern filled with natural gas.

But the ground beneath the drilling rig collapsed, leaving a hole with a diameter of 70 metres. Fearing that the hole would lead to the release of poisonous gases, the team decided to burn it off. It was hoped that the fire would use all the fuel within days, but the gas is still burning today. The flames generate a golden glow which can be seen for miles around Derweze, a village with a population of about 350.

The site is about 260 kilometres north of Ashgabat, the capital of Turkmenistan.

Visitors coming to see "The Door to Hell" can only spend about 5 minutes on average around the site because of the hazardous methane gas the flaming hole produces. It is such a unique sight that many people journey to see the burning crater in the middle of the Karakum Desert.

Would you pay a visit before it is covered up and closed as has been ordered by the Turkmenistan president?

The Principality of Sealand: The World's Smallest Country

During the 1939-45 War, Great Britain established an artificial island on the High Seas. This island was equipped with radar and heavy armaments and occupied by some two hundred servicemen. The task of the island and its inhabitants was to guard the approaches to the Thames Estuary, where large and vulnerable convoys of shipping were assembled.

Sometime after the cessation of hostilities, the island was derelicted and abandoned by the British Government.

Sealand is located in the southern part of the North Sea some six miles off the coast of Britain and from sixty-five to one hundred miles from the coasts of France, Belgium, Holland and Germany; Latitude 51.53 N, Longitude 01.28 E.

But after being abandoned by the Royal Navy in 1956, this artificial island on the high seas has been the site of a pirate radio landing pad, a takeover, a controversial declaration of independence, a coup, and its own miniature war.

In the winter of 1966, a British family took possession and commenced the task of equipping and restoring the island. On 2 September 1967, they hoisted their own flag and declared the existence of a new state - the Principality of Sealand.

In 1967, retired British Army major Paddy Roy Bates occupied the abandoned Rough's Tower in the North Sea, northeast of London and opposite the mouth of the Orwell River and Felixstowe.

Roy Bates had previously operated a low-power station called Radio Essex from another sea barge, but it had been within the 3-mile area of British legal control, and he had been caught and fined. So, he and his 15-year-old son Michael gathered up the equipment, hauled it out to the Roughs Tower, and after a prolonged fight, took over control. But the tower never did become home to pirate radio, as English laws changed soon thereafter to make seaborne pirate transmissions illegal even outside of the 3-mile radius.

Nonetheless, Roy Bates maintained his control of Roughs Tower, and declared it the Principality of Sealand; a sovereign, independent state. This was after consulting with an attorney who found a loophole allowing Roy to claim the fort due to fact that it was in international waters, and that it was up for grabs due to "dereliction of sovereignty." Since it was outside of England's legally controlled area there was nothing the Royal Navy could do about this, but they did demolish another fort that stood beyond the 3-mile boundary, to prevent a similar takeover there.

The following year, the legitimacy of this self-declared state would be put to the test when Michael Bates fired a warning shot at a British Trinity House vessel which approached the tower. This led to Roy Bates' arrest when he next arrived on the mainland. The case against Roy and Michael Bates was brought to court, where the judge ruled that Sealand was outside of British jurisdiction, therefore no ruling could be made against the Bates boys for their actions. The authorities decided not to appeal this ruling, as it may have led to an undesirable precedent.

In 1978 there was a hostage incident on Sealand when a German lawyer named Alexander Achenbach, claiming to be the Prime Minister of Sealand, stormed the sea fort with German and Dutch mercenaries and took Roy Bates' son

Michael hostage. Not long after, Bates was able to retake the tower and captured Achenbach and the mercenaries. Achenbach, a holder of a Sealand passport, was charged with treason by Sealand and was held unless he paid over $35,000 in restitution. The event was important enough to get the German government involved; they had sent a diplomat to Sealand to negotiate a release of Achenbach with Bates. Once freed, Achenbach and his associates returned to Germany and established a "government in exile" of Sealand, still claiming to this day they are the legitimate ruling authority.

Not much exciting has happened there since the miniature war of '78, though Roy was approached by a group of Argentineans during the Falklands War in 1982; they wanted to buy Sealand and set up camp "right on Britain's doorstep." He sent them away.

Why the demand for a dump of a 70-year-old radar station? The international water rights are the key, and it's the laissez-faire attitude most governments take regarding Sealand that drives its appeal: no established government wants to be bothered with the responsibility of servicing and controlling Sealand.

Sealand has been out there ever since, gloriously proclaiming its sovereignty and offering noble titles for $316.54 apiece. Sealand is planning to start its own "multiversity," with a curriculum that would teach how to live on an artificial island. It has a national anthem, "E Mare Libertas", which is really quite a catchy tune.

Perhaps even more bizarre is that Sealand has "national" athletes based all over the world. Sealand has a marathon runner based in Canada, a U-20 soccer team in Kentucky, a competition airsoft team based out of Yorkshire, and a Kung Fu specialist that recently won two silver medals at the World

Cup of Kung Fu.

Sealand has a Destination Imagination team in Dobbs Ferry, New York, a fencing team at UC Irvine, and in 2008 they hosted a Red Bull skateboarding event. They have founded a football association (soccer league). Also, in 2008 the Sealand egg throwing team won the world championship. But not a single athlete competing for Sealand has ever set foot on Sealand, and the current population is estimated to be around 4.

One problem with Sealand is that, as far as artificial islands go, it's kind of, well, what you would expect from a 60-year-old abandoned platform on a couple of concrete pillars out in the middle of the sea -- a bit shabby.

Today, Sealand's sovereignty and legitimacy is not recognized by any traditional States, however it is perhaps the best-known micronation in the world even though its inhabitable area is only 550 square meters. It is quietly tolerated by the UK, which still claims ownership and control of the sandbar upon which Sealand sits.

Sealand's electrical generators are now tasked with powering the servers for HavenCo, a data hosting services company which was started on Sealand in the year 2000. The Bates is leasing the country exclusively to HavenCo Limited, which offers "unparalleled security and independence to users who wish to take advantage of its Internet colocation services."

In 2006, Sealand experienced a fire that quickly consumed the deck. Luckly no one was hurt and the citizens were safely evacuated from the country by the Royal Air Force. Since then, Prince Roy and his wife decided to do what most Royal families do and retire in a foreign country, England. After the move Prince Roy commissioned the Church and East Ltd.

with the task of rebuilding their country.

In 2007 the principality was rumored to be for sale for €750 million. But nothing happened.

If you want to become a citizen of Sealand, you can send your application to-

Principality of Sealand

Diplomatic Mission in the German Reich/Consulate

Postfach 2366

D-14956 Trebbin

Also has its own website- http://www.sealandgov.org/

How to travel to Sealand?

Unless you're planning to swim your way, you'll travel: By helicopter.

Do-

With panoramic views of the Ocean, in Sea land staring at the ocean is a major past time. You could also engage in the famous walking "The Perimeter" or even take part in the ancient ritual of drinking "Tea" which was bought to Sea Land in around 3000 BC by the Ancient Egyptians. Walk, the entire habitable area of the fort is 550 sq.m.

Eat-

Often flounder can be found beached on the platform, this serves as a magnificent feast for the locals. They also engage in the consumption of "microwave dinners"

**There is electricity but no phone connectivity. No smoking or drinking is allowed in the Principality, and no one is allowed more than three five-minute showers per week in the interest of conserving freshwater; much of which is collected from rain. Its population rarely exceeds five people, and in the sake of security, visitors are unwelcome.

Recent development:

Paddy Roy Bates, who occupied an abandoned fort in the North Sea and declared it the sovereign Principality of Sealand with himself as its prince, passed away aged 91 on Oct 9th, 2012.

....

A great setting for a novel, eh!

Racetrack playa

One of the most interesting mysteries of Death Valley National Park is the sliding rocks at Racetrack Playa (a playa is a dry lake bed). These rocks can be found on the floor of the playa with long trails behind them. Somehow these rocks slide across the playa, cutting a furrow in the sediment as they move.

Amid the eerie silence and the 50C heat of California's Death Valley these giant boulders appear to move smoothly - and unaided - across the desert.

The rocks, some as heavy as 17 stone, edge along in bizarre, straight-line patterns across the ultra-flat surface of the valley. They can travel more than 350 yards a year.

That makes the question: "How do they move?" a very challenging one.

Racetrack playa is lake bed that is almost perfectly flat and almost always dry. It is about 4 kilometers long (2.5 miles - north to south) and about 2 kilometers wide (1.25 miles - east to west). The surface is covered with mudcracks and the sediment is made up mainly of silt and clay.

The climate in this area is arid. It rains just a couple of inches per year. However, when it rains, the steep mountains which surround Racetrack Playa produce a large amount of runoff that converts the playa floor into a broad shallow lake. When wet, the surface of the playa is transformed into a very soft and very slippery mud.

Some explanations:

Moved by People or Animals?

The shape of trails behind the rocks suggests that they move during times when the floor of Racetrack Playa is covered with a very soft mud. A lack of disturbed mud around the rock trails eliminates the possibility of a human or animal pushing or assisting the motion of the rocks.

Moved by wind-

This is the favorite explanation. The prevailing winds that blow across Racetrack Playa travel from southwest to northeast. Most of the rock trails are parallel to this direction. This is strong evidence that wind is the prime mover or at least involved with the motion of the rocks.

Strong wind gusts are thought to nudge the rocks into motion. Once the rock begins to move a wind of much lower velocity can keep the rock in motion as it slides across the soft and very slippery mud. Curves in the rock trails are explained by shifts in wind direction or in how the wind interacts with an irregularly shaped rock.

Moved by Ice-

A few people have reported seeing Racetrack Playa covered by a thin layer of ice. One idea is that water freezes around the rocks and then wind, blowing across the top of the ice, drags the ice sheet with its embedded rocks across the surface of the playa.

Some researchers have found highly congruent trails on multiple rocks that strongly support this movement theory. However, the transport of a large ice sheet might be expected to mark the playa surface in other ways - these marks have not been found. Other researchers experimented with stakes that would be disturbed by ice sheets. The rocks moved without disturbing the stakes. The evidence for ice-sheet transport is not consistent.

Moved by gravity-

One early suggestion was that the rocks were driven by gravity, sliding down a gradual slope over a long period of time. But this theory was discounted when it was revealed that the northern end of the playa is actually several centimeters higher than the southern end and that most of the rocks were in fact traveling uphill.

Suggestions:

Some people have suggested attaching radio transmitters to the rocks or erecting cameras to catch them "in the act" in order to put an end to the speculation. But as Death Valley National Park is 95 percent designated wilderness, all research in the park must be noninvasive. It is forbidden to erect any permanent structures or instrumentation. Further, no one is permitted on the playa when it is wet because each footprint would leave an indelible scar.

....

Is it the wind, the ice or Do the giants go bowling there?

UNSOLVED CRIMES

- Jack the Ripper

- The Zodiac Killings

- Black Dahlia

Jack the Ripper

In 1888, THE WORLD'S most famous serial killer stalked the dark, grimy streets of London's East End.

'Jack the Ripper' was the original celebrity mass-murderer, and set a trend for homicidal maniacs which seems to grow with each year.

Unlike many of his modern age copyists, Jack the Ripper was not caught or even named, and to this day it has never been conclusively proven who he really was.

London's Whitechapel district was known as one of the poorest areas of the city, and at the time, was home to over a thousand prostitutes. It was also the area which would become the focus of the Ripper's attacks. His reign of terror officially began in the opening hours of 31st August 1888, when a market porter spotted a woman lying in a doorway on Buck's Row in Whitechapel. Rather than approach the woman, the porter went to find the beat policeman. When he arrived, he found the woman's throat had been deeply cut and a medical examination later revealed her body had been mutilated. Her identity was also discovered: she was Mary Ann Nichols, known as Polly, a 42-year-old prostitute.

Barely a week later, at 6am on 8th September, the body of another woman was found in Hanbury Street, near Buck's Row. She was Annie Chapman, a 45-year-old prostitute whose head had been almost entirely severed from her neck; she had also been disemboweled.

Fear was beginning to spread throughout the community. For the first time in history, the people had a literate public and a scrutinizing press, who were putting the police under a new sort of pressure. Not only were the police there to protect the people of London, they also had to cope with the novel stress of proving their own competence. Just as in modern mass murder cases, the effect of supposition, myths and rumors in newspaper coverage led to a great deal of anxiety. By the time the Ripper struck again, the Whitechapel area was interested in only one thing. The Ripper did not disappoint. In the dark early hours of 30th September, a costume jewellery salesman arrived home in Berners Street, where he discovered the body of Elizabeth Stride, a prostitute who had had her throat slit. As police rushed to the scene and searched the nearby streets, the Ripper made off to Mitre Square, in the City of London, and killed Catharine Eddowes. Although the earlier victim had not been mutilated, many believe the Ripper had been interrupted during this procedure. Eddowes' remains were not so well preserved and she was found disemboweled. This night become known as the 'double event', and was the focus of many letters sent into the police.

Although most came from members of the public offering advice, some purported to come from the Ripper himself and were given more credence than others.

One dated 28th September goaded and teased the police, and was the origin of the name Jack the Ripper, which was how the sender signed off. The second was a postcard dated 1st October and referred to the 'double event' of the night before. The third letter was posted a fortnight later and even included a section of a kidney allegedly removed from Catharine Eddowes. Although the police, as in modern times, had to suspect that these correspondences came from a crank or a hoaxer, the kidney included in the third letter was shrivelled and diseased. An interesting fact is that not only was Eddowes an alcoholic, she also suffered from Bright's disease, and this organ displayed all the signs of being from such an afflicted body. The police believed they had discovered a pattern to the killings the first occurred on 31st August, the second on 8th September, the third and fourth on 30th September. They believed the next would happen on the 8th of October, but in fact the Ripper did not strike for the whole of that month. His final official murder actually occurred on 9th November in Miller's Court, a building close to where the other killings had taken place. Another prostitute, 24-year-old Mary Jane Kelly was found by her landlord with her body utterly mutilated. This time, the murder had taken place inside, and the killer had had all night to dissect the corpse.

Although these five murders are all assigned to the Ripper, there is the possibility he may have killed two or three more woman in London around that time.

However, the police were at a loss to find the real name of the man behind the crimes and employed a policy of information suppression to try to reassure the public. Despite this, Londoners were fully aware that police work was proving fruitless at obtaining a clear picture of the Ripper's identity.

But some of those in the force did have their own theories, and many police doctors who examined the victims' bodies suggested the Ripper was likely to be someone with medical training.

In 1894 the Chief Constable of the Metropolitan Police Force, Sir Melville Macnaghten, wrote a report which named Montague John Druitt, a barrister who committed suicide shortly after the Kelly murder, as the most likely suspect.

However, at the time Macnaghten believed Druitt to be a trained doctor, which subsequent research proved to be false.

Macnaghten also named two more possible Rippers. One was Aaron Kosminski, a Polish Jew who lived in the Whitechapel area and was placed in an insane asylum in March 1889. Although one of the chief investigating officers, Robert Anderson, had a great belief in Kosminski's guilt, the Pole's behavioural records from his time in the asylum contain nothing to suggest he was homicidal.

Macnaghten's final suspect, Michael Ostrog, was a Russian lunatic. Despite being a convicted criminal and possibly having some medical training, his behaviour under studied conditions also did not point to an ability for multiple murders.

In recent years, Ripper investigators have considered Dr Francis Tumblety, an American doctor who fled London shortly after the murders. Despite thinking him a possible suspect, the Metropolitan Police at the time decided to rule him out of it enquires. As with many mysteries, the identity of the Ripper has become the domain of conspiracy theorists.

This has led to people from all walks of life – members of the monarchy, royal servants, high-ranking police officers, Russian spies and even crazed evangelists – being accused of holding the Ripper's identity.

However, in the last few of years a study has been conducted by the crime writer Patricia Cornwell. She used $4million of her own money to investigate if there is a link between the Ripper and Walter Sickert, an impressionist painter who may have had connections with Whitechapel around the dates of the murders. Twenty years after the killings, he created a series of paintings that depicted dead and gruesomely mauled prostitutes. Cornwell has used modern technologies and intense examinations of his work, and is so convinced of Sickert's guilt that she is staking her reputation on him being the Ripper.

Modern Ripper investigators, just like the Victorian London police forces, fail to agree with each other. There were so many unsavory characters roaming London at the time that almost any suspect could have been linked to the murders in some way.

As the years blur the truth, so the plausibility of many different suspects increases, whilst the definitive proof needed to decide on one disappears in the fog of time.

The Zodiac Killer

The Zodiac Killer is one of the great unsolved serial killer mysteries of all time, taking only second place to Jack the Ripper.

Even though police investigated over 2,500 potential suspects, the case was never officially solved.

The Zodiac Killer was a serial killer who stalked parts of Northern California from December 1968 through October 1969. Through a series of cryptic letters, he sent to the press and others, he disclosed his insanity which motivated the killings, offered clues to future murder plots and adopted the name Zodiac.

Before it was all over, this clever and diabolical killer changed the lives of eight people, only two of whom lived to tell the tale.

To this day, police and journalists receive tips on the murders. And there's a thriving cottage industry of enthusiastic amateur Zodiac sleuths, some of whom have devoted their lives to the mystery.

The Zodiac's first claimed murders were in Benicia, Calif., and nearby Vallejo. In both cases the killer pulled up next to a young couple parked in a car and shot them point-blank. Later he stabbed a couple picnicking at Lake Berryessa, in Napa County, and shot a cab driver in San Francisco. He often called police from pay phones to report his crimes.

When it comes to American serial killers, the Zodiac hardly rates. He once hinted that he had killed 37 people, but the confirmed number of his victims is six, spread over late 1968 and 1969.

Yet the Zodiac managed to frighten the entire Bay Area, not merely with his killings but with his threats to blow up school buses or shoot the children as they got off the bus.

Police in Vallejo, where the Zodiac killed three people and wounded another, have long considered the chief suspect to be Arthur Leigh Allen, who died of cancer at age 58 in 1992 without ever being charged. Allen also is the preferred suspect of Robert Graysmith, the former Chronicle political cartoonist whose book on the killings was the foundation for the new movie, "Zodiac."

Police in San Francisco, where the Zodiac killed a cab driver, had their doubts about Allen as a suspect, but the department essentially washed its hands of the case three years ago and now does not talk about it. Mike Rodelli, a New Jersey researcher who has spent nearly 10 years delving into the case and has impressed some longtime Zodiac experts with his findings, is convinced the killer is a well-known San Francisco businessman now in his 80s.

Perhaps the most intriguing theory of what happened to the Zodiac is the one put forward by David Van Nuys, a Sonoma County psychologist who co-authored a book on the killer. Van Nuys believes the Zodiac suffered from multiple personality disorder and got better as the years went along -- and eventually, he simply stopped killing.

"This is the Zodiac speaking," was how he began his letters, which included a distinctive symbol -- two crossed lines through a circle, resembling a telescopic sight's crosshairs.

The papers published the letters and a code that the Zodiac appended to them. In August, a high school teacher in Salinas,

Donald Harden, said he and his wife, Bettye, had cracked the code.

"I like killing people because it is so much fun it is more fun than killing wild game in the forrest," the message said.

His last authenticated letter was to The Chronicle in January 1974, in which he threatened to do "something nasty" if the paper didn't print the message. He signed off, "Me -- 37/SFPD -- 0."

The mystery inspired several films and television shows. Dirty Harry, starring Clint Eastwood is loosely based on the Zodiac case. In 2007, the film Zodiac, starring Jake Gyllenhaal and Robert Downey Jr, focused on police attempts to catch him.

Despite working through 2,500 suspects, the San Francisco Police Department have never caught the killer or even arrested anyone.

Fascinating isn't it. You think you can crack the code?

Black Dahlia

The Black Dahlia is a story that has baffled police and crime buffs for decades now.

On 15 January 1947, the body of 22-year-old Elizabeth Short was found. Short was an attractive, young girl who had arrived in Los Angeles searching for fame as an actress, just as thousands of others do every year. Her demise was to be one of the most gruesome murders America had ever seen.

Elizabeth Short left her hometown of Massachusetts at the age of 16. She arrived in Los Angeles after a few years of drifting from town to town. Short was nicknamed the Black Dahlia because of her jet-black hair and the black clothing that she constantly wore.

On the morning of 15 January, Short's body was found in a deserted lot in South Los Angeles. Her battered torso had been cut in half and sexually assaulted after her death.

The killer taunted investigators. The killer would send little notes that said, "Catch me if you can." There were other woman killed and those murders were never solved as well. Could it be that the other murders were related? Was it possible there was a copycat murder looking for attention? None of the murders were ever solved, even those investigators received numerous confessions that turned out to be false. Is it possible that one of those supposedly false confessions could have been the killer taunting the police another way?

Short's murder quickly became a sensation, not only because of its location in the show biz capital, but also because the police worked in tandem with the press to disseminate clues in hopes of locating a suspect. Several people confessed, only to be later released for lack of evidence. Much speculation surrounded the details of Short's life. Grieving after the death of a man she fell in love with, she reportedly befriended many men while frequenting jazz clubs, making it nearly impossible to pin down who she could have been with before she died.

One former detective, who later became a private investigator, had said that his father George Hodel had committed the murders of Jeanne French and Elizabeth Short. He said that he had the proof, but police ignored the evidence as a way to cover up medical records of some powerful people and police. If George would have been arrested, except police felt he would open up medical records of these people. George left the country never to be heard from again. He died in 1991. His son had asked for the investigation to be reopened. Did this man kill Elizabeth Short? The only people that could know for sure are dead.

Was the unsolved crime covered up and forgotten about because of some powerful people were maybe involved? Was the doctor really the one to kill these two women or was it the son who, was at the time, a detective. He has the evidence to prove his father killed these two women, but nobody wants that information. Was the Elizabeth Short murder related to something we do not even know about? She was only 22 years old. What could be the reason to close her murder file and forget about her?

Nobody knows.

It is surprising that a fifty-year-old murder can still capture our attention today. Though many people still believe the murder will be solved, others believe that the murderer himself has long since passed. If that is true, then we may never know who actually did kill Elizabeth Short.

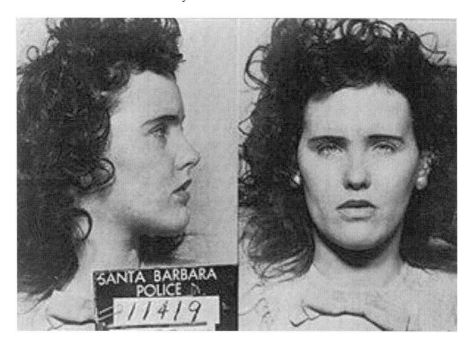

UFO'S / ALIENS / SETI

- *Wow Signal*

- *Betty and Barney Hill: Alien Abduction*

- *Roswell Incident*

- *Area 51*

- *Cumberland Spaceman*

- *Marfa Lights*

WOW Signal

The 'Wow! signal' was received at 11.16pm on August 15, 1977 - the night before Elvis died - as a radio telescope in Ohio swept its gaze through the constellation of Sagittarius. In Ohio, a 37-year-old man named Jerry Ehman was transfixed by another startling event that—at least for searchers for extraterrestrial intelligence—potentially was even more momentous.

Ehman, a volunteer researcher for Ohio State University's now-defunct Big Ear radio observatory, pebrused data from the telescope's scan of the skies on August 15, a few days earlier. In those days, such information was run through an IBM 1130 mainframe computer and printed on perforated paper, and then laboriously examined by hand. But the tedium was shattered when Ehman spotted something surprising—a vertical column with the alphanumerical sequence "6EQUJ5," which had occurred at 10:16 p.m. EST. He grabbed a red pen and circled the sequence. In the margin, wrote "Wow!"

Ehman's excitement over that bit of arcane information stemmed from the Big Ear's mission at the time, which was searching space for radio signals of the sort that might be emanated by extraterrestrial civilizations, if they were attempting to make contact with intelligent life elsewhere in the universe. To Ehman, this signal, which had come from the direction of the constellation Sagittarius, looked an awful lot like it could be such a message.

Two aspects of this signal immediately caught the attention of Ehman and project director John Kraus, who saw the results the following morning.

First of all, 37 seconds was precisely the time it takes the Big Ear scanning beam to survey a given point in the heavens.

Because of this, any signal coming from space would follow precisely the "Wow!" signal's pattern - increasing and then decreasing over 37 seconds. This practically ruled out the possibility that the signal was the result of Earthly radio interference.

Secondly, the signal was not continuous, but intermittent.

Kraus and Ehman knew that, because Big Ear has two separate beams that scan the same area of the sky in succession, several minutes apart. But the signal appeared on only one of the beams and not on the other, indicating that it had been 'turned off' between the two scans. A strong, focused, and intermittent signal coming from outer space: could it be that Big Ear had detected an alien signal?

But was it sent by an advanced civilization?

Curiously, the signal was picked up by only one of the scope's two detectors. When the second detector covered the same patch of sky three minutes later, it heard nothing. This indicated either the unlikely possibility that the first beam had detected something that wasn't there, or that the source of the signal had been shut off or redirected in the intervening time. The observatory researchers trained their massive scope on that part of the sky for a full month, watching closely for a repeat of the mysterious signal.

Nothing interesting was observed during those thirty days, yet scientists were at a loss for an explanation of the original event. Planning to return to that patch of sky periodically, the Big Ear continued its broader purpose.

Several times over the next twenty years, longtime SETI researcher Robert Gray and his colleague Kevin B. Marvel arranged for further scans of that region of space. They managed to obtain some time on the META array at the Oak Ridge Observatory in Massachusetts, and the extremely sensitive Very Large Array (VLA) in New Mexico, which is made up of twenty-seven 25-meter radio dishes. They detected some extremely faint sources of radio emissions in the infamous patch of sky, but nothing like that of the "Wow!" signal.

"Wow" remains the strongest and clearest signal ever received from an unknown source in space, as well as the most fascinating and unexplainable. The signal's original discoverer Jerry Ehman doesn't care to speculate on its source, and he remains scientifically skeptical.

"Even if it were intelligent beings sending a signal," he said in an interview, "they'd do it far more than once. We should have seen it again when we looked for it 50 times."

What was it? A miscommunication or something else.

Betty and Barney Hill: Alien Abduction:

It was shortly before midnight on September 19, 1961 when Betty and Barney Hill had the experience which was to shape all of modern alien folklore. They were driving from Canada to Portsmouth, New Hampshire. Near the resort of Indian Head, New Hampshire, they stopped their car in the middle of Route 3 to observe a strange light moving through in the sky. The next thing they knew, they were about 35 miles further along on their trip, and several hours had elapsed.

Betty telephoned their close friend, Major Paul Henderson at nearby Pease Air Force Base, to report a UFO sighting. Major Henderson found that this was corroborated by two separate UFO reports from radar data from two different Air Force installations nearby. All three reports are officially recorded in Project Blue Book. Then Betty began having nightmares two weeks later. In her nightmares, she described being taken aboard an alien spacecraft and having medical experiments performed. As a result of these nightmares, Betty and Barney decided to undergo hypnosis. In separate sessions, they described nearly identical experiences of being taken on board the alien spacecraft by what we now call gray aliens: Short beings with huge black eyes and smooth gray skin. Both of the Hills had a whole spectrum of tests done. Betty was shown a star map which she was able to memorize and reproduce later, and which has been identified as showing Zeta Reticuli as the aliens' home planet. After the experiments they were taken back to their car in a dazed condition, and sent along their way.

Innumerable books and movies were made about the Betty & Barney Hill abduction. It was the introduction of the gray alien into popular culture. It was also the beginning of the entire "alien abduction" phenomenon. The physical evidence of the star map and the radar reports are said to have both withstood all scrutiny.

Much of the Hill story is said to be based on these separate hypnosis sessions. In fact, that turns out not to be the case at all. It's important to note that it was more than two years after the incident that the Hills underwent hypnosis. During those two years, Betty was writing and rewriting her accounts of her dreams. All of the significant details you may have heard about the Hills' medical experiments came from Betty's two years of writings: A long needle inserted into her navel; the star map; the aliens' fascination with Barney's dentures; the examination of both Betty and Barney's genitals; and the overall chronology of the episode, including being met on the ground by the aliens, a leader coming forward and escorting them to exam rooms, the aliens' general demeanor and individual personalities, and the way they spoke to Betty in English but to Barney via telepathy. Betty wrote all of this based only on what she claims were her dreams, and probably told the story to Barney over and over again until his ears fell off over a period of two years, before they ever had any hypnosis.

During those two years, Barney's own recollection was somewhat less dramatic. When they first saw the light in the sky, Betty said she thought it was a spacecraft, but Barney always said he thought it was an airplane.

When Betty was aboard the craft, she stated she was shown a star map, and was asked by one of the humanoids, "Where are you on the map?" to which she shrugged and said, "I don't know."

However, approximately 8 years thereafter, when more powerful telescopes came into use, several scientists claim to have found a match for this map.

Being intrigued with the mystery of the map, (which Betty drew from hypnosis), an Ohio schoolteacher and amateur astronomer Marjorie Fish became involved in the case in 1969.

Betty drew the stars from her memory and presented to her.

Astronomers at Ohio State University had a computer put them in their exact position out beyond the double star system of Zeta Reticuli 1 and Zeta Reticuli 2--220 trillion miles, 37 light years from earth, looking toward our sun. The computer duplicated with virtually no variation, the map of Betty Hill.

The Betty & Barney Hill abduction story has every indication of being merely an inventive tale from the mind of a lifelong UFO fanatic. Was it an illusion, a ploy to get popularity or a real UFO abduction?

Roswell Incident

A controversial series of events that occurred in Roswell New Mexico in 1947 in which the US military allegedly recovered the crashed remains of an extraterrestrial spacecraft and its occupants and then covered the whole thing up. To this day the event remains one of the most popular conspiracy theories with references appearing in film, books and media.

One morning around Independence Day 1947, about 75 miles from the town of Roswell, New Mexico, a rancher named Mac Brazel found something unusual in his sheep pasture: a mess of metallic sticks held together with tape; chunks of plastic and foil reflectors; and scraps of a heavy, glossy, paper-like material. Unable to identify the strange objects, Brazel called Roswell's sheriff. The sheriff, in turn, called officials at the nearby Roswell Army Air Force base. Soldiers fanned out across Brazel's field, gathering the mysterious debris and whisking it away in armored trucks.

(Early in July, 1947, after hearing about Arnold's "flying saucers", ranch foreman Mac Brazel told the Sheriff of Chaves County about some strange material he had found on the Foster Ranch, and that he was sure it was the remains of a "flying disk". Sheriff Wilcox passed this information on to the Roswell Army Air Force base and the base intelligence officer, Major Jessie Marcel, was immediately detailed to look into the matter.)

On July 8, "RAAF Captures Flying Saucer on Ranch in Roswell Region" was the top story in the Roswell Daily Record. But was it true? On July 9, an Air Force official clarified the paper's report: The alleged "flying saucer," he said, was only a crashed weather balloon. However, to anyone who had seen the debris (or the newspaper photographs of it), it was clear that whatever this thing was, it was no weather balloon. Some people believed–and still believe–that the crashed vehicle had not come from Earth at all. They argued that the debris in Brazel's field must have come from an alien spaceship.

Locals who had witnessed the strange material were threatened by the military not to disclose what they had seen. Nurses working at the local hospital reported even stranger things, many of them claimed to have seen the military corner off a section of the building. The nurses who were permitted to enter the area witnessed what they described as "little men" - small humanoid bodies which were being examined by medical personnel. There were even reports that one of the humanoid creatures was still alive and walking around. Nurses working in this area later claimed to have been sick for a long time afterwards due to the toxic smell that was present there. It wasn't long before the strange bodies were moved from the hospital to an unknown location. The Roswell Incident was becoming one of the greatest cover ups in history.

One retired soldier claimed to have been taken out to the site of the Roswell Crash at the time the incident occurred. He claimed to have witnessed a strange metallic craft embedded in the hillside, and several strange bodies littered around the crash site. Inside the craft he reported seeing strange controls and symbols carved into the metal as well as further bodies which had been thrown out of the craft as a result of the impact.

Dummy Drops and UFOs

These skeptics grew during the 1950s, when the Air Force

conducted a series of secret "dummy drops" over air bases, test ranges and unoccupied fields across New Mexico. These experiments, meant to test ways for pilots to survive falls from high altitudes, sent bandaged, featureless dummies with latex "skin" and aluminum "bones"–dummies that looked an awful lot like space aliens were supposed to–falling from the sky onto the ground, whereupon military vehicles would descend on the landing site to retrieve the "bodies" as quickly as possible. To people who believed the government was covering up the truth about the Roswell landing, these dummy drops seemed just as suspicious. They were convinced that the dummies were actually extraterrestrial creatures who were being kidnapped and experimented on by government scientists.

Roswell and the Mysterious Project Mogul

It turned out that the Army knew more about Brazel's "flying saucer" than it let on. Since World War II, a group of geophysicists and oceanographers from Columbia University, New York University and the Woods Hole Oceanographic Institution on Cape Cod had been working on a top-secret atomic espionage project at New Mexico's Alamogordo Air Field that they called Project Mogul. Project Mogul used sturdy high-altitude balloons to carry low-frequency sound sensors into the tropopause, a faraway part of the Earth's atmosphere that acts as a sound channel. In this part of the atmosphere, sound waves can travel for thousands of miles without interference, much like under the ocean. The scientists believed that if they sent microphones into this sound channel, they would be able to eavesdrop on nuclear tests as far away as the Soviet Union.

According to the U.S. military, the debris in Brazel's field outside Roswell actually belonged to Project Mogul. It was the remains of a 700-foot-long string of neoprene balloons, radar reflectors (for tracking) and sonic equipment that the scientists had launched from the Alamogordo base in June and that had, evidently, crashed in early July 1947. Because the project was highly classified, no one at the Roswell Army Air Field even knew that it existed, and they had no idea what to make of the objects Brazel had found. The "weather balloon" story, flimsy though it was, was the simplest and most plausible explanation they could come up with on short notice. Meanwhile, to protect the scientists' secret project, no one at Alamogordo could step in and clear up the confusion.

Roswell Today

Today, many people continue to believe that the government and the military are covering up the truth about alien landings at and around Roswell. In 1994, the Pentagon declassified most of its files on Project Mogul and the dummy drops, and the federal General Accounting Office produced a report ("Report of Air Force Research Regarding the Roswell Incident") designed to debunk these rumors. Nevertheless, there are still people who subscribe to the UFO theory, and hundreds of thousands of curiosity seekers visit Roswell and the crash site every year, hoping to find out the truth for themselves.

Area 51

Area 51 is situated in the southwestern portion of Lincoln County in southern Nevada in the western United States. A large military airfield is situated at its center. This center is known as the most secretive places in the world. Although, the base's primary purpose as explained by the authorities is to support development and testing of experimental aircraft and weapons systems, there are thousands of people who do not believe this story.

The intense secrecy surrounding the base, the very existence of which the US Government barely acknowledges, together with reports of unusual phenomena has led it to become the frequent subject of conspiracy theories and UFO folklore.

There are many stories circulating around on Area 51 - most of them are about UFOs and aliens.

1. Alien spacecraft storage: Storage, examination, and reverse engineering of crashed alien spacecraft

2. Study of aliens: Examination of dead aliens that came in UFOs and interrogation of living aliens

3. Manufacture of aircraft based on alien technology

4. Meetings or joint undertakings with extraterrestrials

5. Energy weapons: Development of exotic energy weapons said to be many times deadlier

6. Weather control: Established means of weather control

or experiments undergoing over it

7. Time travel: Established means of time travel or development of time travel technology

8. Aurora aircraft: Development of unusual and exotic propulsion systems related to the Aurora Aircraft Program (a cutting age spy plane)

9. Politics and secret society: Activities related to a supposed shadowy one world government and/or the Majestic Twelve organization (A secret committee of scientists, military leaders, and government officials, supposedly formed in 1947 by an executive order of U.S. President Harry S. Truman to investigate UFO activity)

10. Simulation of moon's environment: In 2000-2001, Fox Television broadcast a show about Apollo moon landing hoax accusations, in which it was suggested that the entire moon landing in 1969 was a hoax and was filmed in parts of Area 51

11. Misdirection attempt: During the mid-1990s, the most secret work previously done in Area 51 was quietly moved to other facilities and the continued secrecy around is largely a successful attempt at misdirection

Proofs

1. In 1989, Bob Lazar claimed that he had worked at a facility at Papoose Lake Lake (which he called S-4) on such a U.S. Government flying saucer.

2. The 1996 documentary Dreamland directed by Bruce Burgess included an interview with a 71 year old mechanical engineer who claimed to be a former employee at Area 51 during the 1950s, working on a "flying disc simulator" built to train US Pilots, based on a disc originating from a crashed

extraterrestrial craft. During his career at Area 51 he claimed to have worked with an extraterrestrial being whose name was "J-Rod", described as a telepathic translator.

3. Dan Burisch (real name, Dan Crain) claims to have worked on cloning alien viruses at Area 51, also with the alien "J-Rod".

4. In July 1996, a man named "Victor" announced on Art Bell's Coast to Coast AM radio show that he had a videotape of an alien interrogation which had taken place in Area 51. He claimed that he had made a copy of the tape during a scheduled transfer of analogue videotape files on the base into digital form, and had then smuggled the copy out of Area 51. The video appears to show the head of an alien creature in a dark interrogation room, allegedly using telepathy to communicate with military personnel and scientists. The footage was eventually included in a video documentary entitled Area 51: The Alien Interview.

Theories:

Some believe that an alien spacecraft crashed in Roswell, New Mexico, and that the government shipped the wreckage and a body to Area 51 for examination and study. A few go even further, claiming the facility has underground levels and tunnels connecting it to other secret sites, and that it contains warehouses full of alien technology and even living alien specimens.

Some theorize that the aliens are actually the ones running the show and that their goal is to create a human-alien hybrid. Stories cast the aliens in roles from benevolent visitors to evil overlords who subsist on a paste made from ground-up human bits.

Air Force representatives have publicly denied that aliens

have anything at all to do with Area 51, but that seems to have only strengthened conspiracy theorists' wilder suggestions.

June 24, 1947, was the day the term flying saucer entered the American vocabulary. That was the day Kenneth Arnold reported sighting a UFO while piloting his private plane over Washington state. He said the object flew like a saucer would if you skipped it across the water, and the flying saucer was born.

On July 8, 1947, Roswell Army Air Field issued a press release written by General William "Butch" Blanchard, stating they had recovered the remains of an unidentified flying object. The Army quickly retracted the statement, but not before it ran in several papers. According to the Army, it was not a flying disc at all, but a weather balloon. Years later, declassified documents said that the object recovered at Roswell was actually a balloon created for a surveillance program called Project Mogul. The weather balloon story was a cover for this secret project. Of course, UFO believers say that the spy balloon story is also a cover, and that the Army really did recover an alien craft.

Reverse Engineering-

In 1987, a man named Robert Lazar shocked the world when he went on television claiming to have been part of an operation that worked on alien technology. Robert Lazar said that the government has possession of at least nine alien spacecraft at a base called S-4, which is not far from Groom Lake.

The facility even had posters showing a UFO levitating several feet above the ground with the caption "They're Here!"

EG&G hired him to help reverse engineer the technology

in the alien craft for use in U.S. military vehicles and power production. He discovered a rusty, heavy substance he called "Element 115" that powered the alien spacecraft.

Skeptics have thoroughly investigated as many of Lazar's statements as they can, and many of them appear to be false. For example, Lazar says he holds Masters degrees from CalTech and MIT, but there's no evidence he ever attended either university. Lazar says this is because the government is actively trying to erase his existence to discredit him. Skeptics believe Lazar is merely fabricating the entire story, and point out that it's a monumental task to erase someone's identity — they would have to remove Lazar's name in everything from official documents to school yearbooks. Even so, Lazar's statements inspired an explosion of interest in UFOs and Area 51.

Secret Organization, MJ12-

One claim common to Lazar's statements and other UFO enthusiasts' theories is a secret organization known as MJ-12, sometimes called Majestic or Majic 12. This group originally included a dozen extremely powerful individuals like President Harry S. Truman, the heads of organizations like the CIA and powerful businessmen.

Many documents reported to be from this group have surfaced, mostly as discoveries of UFOlogist William L. Moore, including papers bearing Presidential signatures. Skeptics scrutinized these documents and uncovered many signs that they are fakes, including proof that signatures were copied from other official documents and pasted onto the MJ-12 papers. Conspiracy theorists denounce the skeptics as either being fooled or actually employed by the government. Other theorists say the MJ-12 documents are fakes, but were official fakes made by the government to throw people off track. Most believers fall into one of several groups, and often each group will accuse the others of actively promoting disinformation to hide the truth.

The most extreme theories about aliens at Area 51 state that not only are aliens here on Earth, they're running the show. Stories circulate about extraterrestrial biological entities (EBEs) forcing the government into agreements that always turn out bad for the rest of us. According to them, the government has agreed to allow aliens to abduct people at will, experiment on helpless citizens and even grind people up into a paste that is later smeared onto EBEs as a source of nutrition. Other theorists say that the aliens are here to use humans to create a hybrid creature, and that the aliens themselves are no longer able to reproduce on their own. Some offer hope with reports of shootouts between government forces and aliens, resulting in the return of our government to power. Of course, almost all of these theorists suggest the government is acting in wicked and irresponsible ways with the citizens of the United States emerging as the ultimate victims.

Hangar 18-

In UFO enthusiast lore, Hangar 18 is the name of the building that houses a captured alien spacecraft and even an extraterrestrial being. The location of Hangar 18 is up for debate among believers. Some have claimed the hangar at Area 51 is Hangar 18. A film titled "Area 51: The Alien Interview" shows an alleged alien in captivity, though skeptics raised doubts of its authenticity. Rick Baker, a special effects expert with many years of experience, stated categorically that he believed the alien to be nothing more than a puppet.

Spot to watch UFO's-

Because the airspace around and above Area 51 is used for test flights and training missions, it is quite possible (and even probable) that you'll see aircraft flying overhead. Sometimes that aircraft might be exotic, perhaps even unidentifiable to the untrained eye. Even familiar aircraft might fool you into thinking you've seen something not of this Earth. Skeptics point out that many reported UFO sightings coincide conveniently with the scheduled daily arrival of the Janet flights to the base. Many of the formerly classified projects at Area 51 really do look to be otherworldly. UAVs (Unmanned Aerial Vehicles) in particular seem strange, as they don't require a cockpit or doors. In addition, many training exercises use bright flares to draw off missile fire or even just to distract onlookers while secret aircraft go through maneuvers. A popular spot to watch for UFOs is the Black Mailbox on Nevada Highway 375. The mailbox belongs to a local rancher and became famous when Lazar said it was the location, he'd bring people to in order to watch scheduled test flights of alien spacecraft. Today, the mailbox has been repainted white and the rancher has said many times that he doesn't believe any of the craft flying overhead are alien in origin.

Whether you believe it being the military area or the UFO harbor, it is definitely intriguing and mysterious.

Cumberland Spaceman

In 1964, a man named Jim Templeton took a photograph of his young daughter while visiting Burgh Marsh in Cumberland, a county in northwest England. After Kodak developed the picture, Templeton was stunned to see what appears to be a white figure standing behind his daughter. Templeton claims that he did not see anyone in the background while he was taking the photograph, but does recall that some animals in the area were behaving strangely at the time.

Kodak investigated the film and did not find any evidence of tampering. Templeton claimed that he was later visited by two government agents in dark suits (similar to the "men in black" tales often associated with alleged witnesses of UFO's). They supposedly attempted to intimidate him into admitting that his photo depicted nothing unusual. The picture quickly captured the public's imagination. Jim Templeton died in 2011 at the age of 91, still insisting that the photo is genuine. Who, or what, is the figure depicted behind young Elizabeth Templeton?

Theories –

-Templeton hoaxed the photograph. A friend or family member dressed up in a costume and stood behind his daughter.

-The photo depicts someone wearing a cloaking device, possibly as part of a secret government experiment.

-The spaceman was an alien, a ghost, or an entity from a parallel universe.

Marfa Lights

So-called ghost lights, also known as spook lights, have been reported in many parts of the world.

One of the most famous havens for ghost lights is the rural town of Marfa, Texas. Sightings of the Marfa Lights reportedly go back as far as the 19thcentury. They have been witnessed by countless people and studied by scientists.

There is no doubt that the Marfa Lights exist, but what causes them? The television program "Unsolved Mysteries" featured a segment about the lights and conducted an on-screen interview with a man who had seen the lights at a remote Marfa army base during the 1940's, when there was no significant traffic in the area. Despite this, the most common conventional explanation for the Marfa lights (and most ghost lights) is that they are caused by car light reflections. There are also many other theories, ranging from scientific to paranormal.

Theories

-The lights are caused by automobile light reflections. Proponents of this theory usually dismiss all pre-traffic sightings as hoaxes and lies.

-They are will-o-the-wisp, St. Elmo's fire, refracted starlight, or swamp gas.

-They are a mirage caused by the area's atmospheric conditions.

-They are ball lightning.

-Witnesses are seeing campfires in the distance and mistaking them for something unusual.

-The lights are UFO's. Apparently, the aliens have been flying in the same area for several decades. They must be pretty bored by now.

-The lights are the spirits of the dead. There is a Native American legend that the ghost of an Apache chief still haunts the area. There are also local legends in many spooklight areas about a man who was decapitated in a train accident. The ghost light is supposedly the lantern his spirit uses to search for his severed head.

Choose the one, you love the most.

PREVIEW VOL. 2

Volume two of "Strangest Mysteries Of The World And Beyond" contains the following topics:

Ancient Aliens
Sumerian Culture And The Anunnaki
Moon And Ancient Aliens
Baalbek, "Landing Place" Of An Ancient Race Of Aliens
Mystery Of Crop Circles

Strangest Disappearances
Aemelia Earhart
The Eilean Mor Mystery
Death Of Adolf Hitler

Strangest Customs And Traditions
Bouncing Babies
Foot Binding
The Bird And The Bees
The Hanging Coffin
Catalan Defecator
Yanomamis- Dead Eating Tribe
Blackening Of The Bride
Polterabend
Strangest Courtship Rituals

Seers And Their Predictions
Nostradamus And His Predictions

Strange Cults
Aghori
Raelism: The Ufo Cult

Strangest Conspiracies
Moon Landing Conspiracy?
Is Paul Dead?
Reptilian Humanoids
Is Elvis Alive?
The Philadelphia Experiment

Strangest Coincidences
Titan And Titanic
Lincoln And J.F. Kennedy
Cannibalistic Coincidence
The War Begins In The Front Yard And Ends In The Front Parlour
Crossword Puzzles Revealed D-Day Code Names In Advance
Did World War 1 Start Over A Sandwich?
A Novel That Unsuspectedly Described The Spy Next Door
The Same Book
King Umberto I Meets His Double
Mark Twain And Halley's Comet

Strangest Human Mysteries
Spontaneous Human Combustion
Is There Hidden Meaning In What We Say, If We Say It Backwards?
Weird Rain
Weird Clouds

Strangest Laws
Silly Ohio Laws

Strangest Truths About Fairy Tales Or Gory Tales
Fairy Tales Or Gory Tales

Hidden Sex*Al Messages In Cartoons

Dark And Sinister Origins Of Nursery Rhymes

Bizarre Love Rituals

Mystery Of The Curses
The Curse Of The Hope Diamond
The Curse Of King Tut
The Curse Of Macbeth
Winchester Mystery House Curse
Bruce And Brandon Lee- Curse Or Planned Murders?
Curse Of James Dean's Little Bast*Rd
Tecumseh's Curse
The Curse Of The Crying Boy
The Curse Of The "Poltergeist" Trilogy

To purchase visit the following link:

https://www.amazon.com/dp/B08MSRC5HK

ABOUT THE AUTOR

Edward Collins is a historian, investigator and writer. His passion for discovering the unknown has led him to create works about mysteries and discoveries in the world.

Today he is more determined than ever to share his extensive research and discoveries, through his books, lectures and business.

His latest major release is the book: *Darkest Unsolved Mysteries: From The Netflix Series 'Unsolved Mysteries'*

For more information on the book visit the following link:
https://www.amazon.com/dp/B08KH47ZQL

EDWARD COLLINS